The Kitchen Gardener's Cookbook

The Kitchen Gardener's Cookbook

Written by Michelle Gillett
Illustrated by Gerry McElroy

Country Roads Press
Oaks, Pennsylvania

Illustrations by Gerry McElroy
Typesetting by Free Hand Press, Inc.

Copyright © 1996 by Michelle Gillett
Published by Country Roads Press
2170 West Drive
P.O. Box 838
Oaks, Pennsylvania 19456

Library of Congress Cataloging-in-Publication Data

Gillett, Michelle.
The Kitchen Gardener's Cookbook / Michelle Gillett.
p.   cm.
Includes index.
ISBN 1-56626-163-5 (pbk. : alk. paper)

1. Cookery (Vegetables) 2. Gardening. I. Title.
TX801.G55 1996   641.6'5--dc20

Printed in Canada

96-18780
CIP

Contents

- INTRODUCTION 1
- COOKING METHODS 3
- PART I: SPRING
  - Peas 11
  - Radishes 14
  - Spring Onions, Leeks, and Garlic 15
  - Asparagus 19
  - Parsnips 22
  - Beets 23
  - Chard 25
- PART II: EARLY SUMMER
  - Green Beans 32
  - Broccoli 36
  - Carrots 39
  - Eggplant 42
  - Cauliflower 45
  - Greens 47
- PART III: SUMMER
  - Cucumbers 58
  - Tomatoes 61
  - Zucchini 68
  - Corn 70
  - Peppers 74
  - Spinach 78
  - Potatoes 80
  - Cabbage 84
- PART IV: FALL
  - Root Vegetables 92
  - Winter Squash and Pumpkins 94
  - Brussels Sprouts 97
  - Dried Beans and Shelling Beans 99
- PART V: HERBS AND EDIBLE FLOWERS 103
- INDEX 119

Introduction

This cookbook offers a collection of easy-to-prepare recipes made from garden-grown vegetables. It also provides tips and facts about harvesting, planting, and preparing vegetables and herbs from a kitchen garden. The book is organized according to planting and growing seasons. Many of the recipes can be added to or adapted. Meat, fish, poultry, and other combinations of vegetables can enhance many of the dishes, especially pasta and grain recipes. Many of the herbs can be mixed with butter for interesting sandwich spreads, added to vinegars, or mixed together to add to dressings and sauces.

Sue Dunlaevy and Elizabeth Baer, both seasoned and expert vegetable growers, helped with the growing and cooking information and contributed recipes to this book. Sue grew up on a fruit farm and has one of the most wonderful kitchen gardens I have ever seen. When she comes in from working in her gardens, she is much too tired to prepare anything complicated for dinner. She taught me that kitchen-garden recipes should be simple and straightforward. The flavors of the garden don't need much improvement or embellishment. Elizabeth believes in growing what she can't find at the local farm stands. She has discovered that there is an enormous difference in flavor in home-grown dried or shelling beans and those bought from the store. Her planting and growing experiments were a resource for this book.

Kitchen gardens are extensions of our houses. We want to walk out the door and be able to snip some parsley or chives, pick beans or corn, or pluck a pepper or two. The menu for an evening meal often reveals itself in a late-afternoon assessment of what is ripe. Like summer itself, the kitchen garden is a place that lures us out of our houses. When we return, we are laden with its gifts.

Methods for Cooking Vegetables

Blanching: Bring a large saucepan of cold water to rolling boil over high heat. Immerse vegetables briefly in boiling water, until their color brightens, but they are still crisp.

Steaming: Vegetables can be placed in a steamer over a saucepan of water, or in a little water. The water must be boiling before the vegetables are added. The steamer or saucepan must be covered while the vegetables are cooking.

Microwaving: Most fresh vegetables can be cooked in a microwave. The process is similar to steaming. Place the vegetables in a microwave proof dish, add a small amount of water, cover tightly with plastic wrap, and cook for 3 to 5 minutes.

Grilling: Vegetables should be at room temperature. Cook the vegetables on a clean, well-oiled grill that has been preheated for at least 5 minutes. Turn them with tongs to ensure cooking on all sides. Vegetables will be soft when done. Do not overcook. Serve grilled vegetables immediately.

Stir-frying: Slice vegetables on the diagonal and cut into bite-sized pieces. Heat the wok or skillet and add about 2 tablespoons of cooking oil. Cook seasonings first. Remove them from the wok or skillet before stir-frying the vegetables so that they do not get over-cooked. Return the seasonings when vegetables are nearly done. Add the longest-cooking vegetables first. Add a little liquid to avoid sticking.

Spring

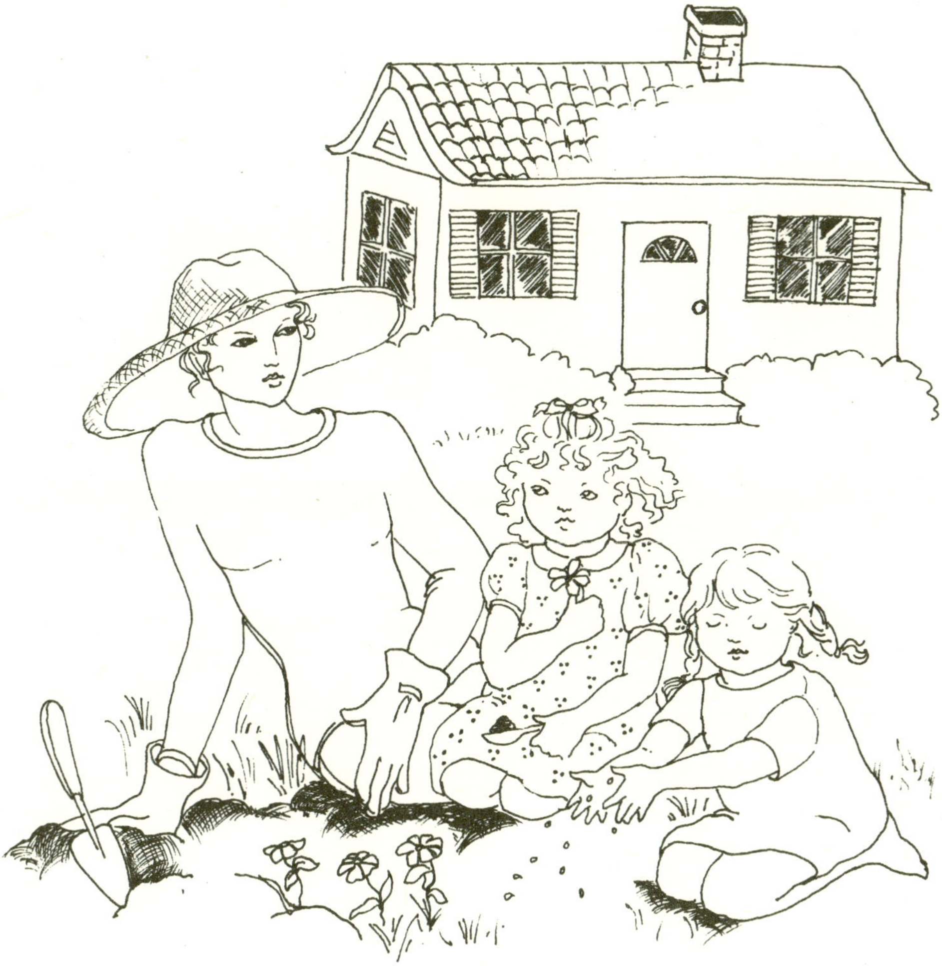

The Kitchen Gardener's Cookbook

☙ Spring

In the suburbs where I grew up, people in our neighborhood did not grow vegetables. Patios and porches displayed pots of orange-red geraniums with horsy-smelling leaves. My mother grew roses and planted beds of pink and white petunias. In the summer, we bought vegetables from the farmstand down the street. The rest of the year, we ate supermarket salads: iceberg lettuce, pallid tomatoes, waxy cucumbers. My mother, who is English, was critical of American produce; it didn't compare with English farm-grown fare. BB-sized peas and thick, mealy string beans never found their way to our table; my mother would buy canned petit pois or frozen French-cut beans before subjecting her family to tasteless or tough vegetables. In spite of her cooking knowledge, my mother had no interest in growing her own vegetables, an enterprise she associated with World War II and victory gardens and rationing.

I didn't get introduced to growing vegetables until I went to stay with my English grandmother during my childhood summers. Until the war, my grandmother had been a city person. The war forced her and my grandfather and their six children to relocate from London to a rural village in Buckinghamshire, where necessity turned my grandmother into a gardener. She had a family to feed in wartime. She also raised chickens and rabbits to ensure nutrition for her family. The war gave my grandmother a passion for gardening that she pursued into her old age. My first impression of a kitchen garden was the eccentric plan that ruled her property at her cottage in Hertfordshire. Cabbages and lettuce filled the spaces between fragrant rose bushes. Picking salad greens was fraught with danger. While the rose blooms perfumed the air above my head, their thorny stems threatened my bare arms and hands. The chicken coop and rabbit hutch at the bottom of the garden invited me to traverse the lawn between the wide rows of vegetables and flowers. I would pet the soft rabbits in their hay-lined hutch, pull eggs from the sour-smelling coop. The chickens escaped with regularity and my grandmother would send me, her American suburban granddaughter whose experience with live chickens was confined to petting zoos, to round them up. I would run around the yard making clucking noises, hoping one of the flapping, scurrying creatures would rush into my arms. Occasionally, I managed to corner one and wrestle it into submission.

When I was young and newly married, I modeled my garden after

The Kitchen Gardener's Cookbook

my grandmother's. I planted tomatoes and lettuce in the perennial beds of our small yard in New Jersey. But I was so busy taking care of babies, I didn't have much time to tend my crops. The snapdragons crowded the tomatoes. If I neglected to water, seedlings shriveled up and vanished into the dirt. The lettuce developed a couple of sickly yellow leaves no larger than the rose petals that loomed on blooms above them. It seemed I did not possess my grandmother's green thumb and sense of eccentric symmetry. Several years later, my husband and I and two small daughters moved to Western Massachusetts. We settled into our house in December, so I had no idea what I would find in the garden when the snow melted. When I walked out in March to investigate my property, my grandmother's memory accompanied me. A rectangular vegetable garden occupied the side yard and abutted the empty lot next door where a neighbor kept his rabbits.

We were ambitious with that first garden. My husband wanted to grow corn. I cared more about salads and beans and peas and tomatoes. The girls were definite about including pumpkins in our patch of earth. We filled every inch of tilled and fertilized soil with seeds and seedlings. Our first harvest was more abundant than I had either imagined or desired. I had no idea that a small garden could yield so many zucchinis or that they grew to be as large as newborns. I was not proficient at pickling or putting up anything. So the zucchinis became decorative objects for the kitchen until we managed to donate them to protesting visitors. We ate lots of spaghetti in those days, so not too many tomatoes rotted or traveled in car trunks back to New York or the suburbs. A neighbor showed me how to make and can tomato sauce, enabling us to vary our summer diet a little. I learned how to dry and freeze and store.

I remember that first spring in our first house and garden more clearly than any of the other growing seasons that have come and gone since. While I turned the soil, my two daughters, aged two and four, armed with miniature gardening tools and kitchen spoons, dug happily beside me. They would travel back and forth from visiting the rabbits to digging for worms. They embraced the tasks I gave them with an enthusiasm I struggled to recall years later when they languished in the house as adolescents, disdainful of anything that grew or was attended by the adjective "fresh" unless it was behavior.

But in those early days, they would crouch to drop seeds in the furrows I made, then per my instructions, push and pat the dirt over

Spring

the rows. At the end of our labors, we would trail into the house, dirty and contented. Daily, they checked for the appearance of leaves and blossoms. Their eagerness to pick the fruits of our labor meant everything we ate was "early" or "baby" long before baby vegetables were considered gourmet food items. I fantasized about harvesting fully grown squash and greens. The girls pulled carrots and radishes, plucked peas and beans, and tried to restrain themselves from picking the tomatoes before they were ripe. They kept vigil by the lengthening vines at the far end of the garden for signs of the Great Pumpkin. I weeded and mulched and watered. It was one of those rare times in life when order was achievable, when the days were as simple and defined as the tidy rows I tended.

Peas

Growing Tip: Peas are meant to grow in cold weather. As soon as you can rototill the ground, plant the peas 1 1/2 inches apart and 1 1/2 inches deep. If you plant peas in early May, they will be ready to pick in June. Tall peas are usually the sweetest and do best when they are upright. Use stakes and chicken wire to support them.

Freezing Tip: Shell the peas and scald them in boiling water for 1 minute. Drain and run under cold water to chill. Place the peas in storage bags and freeze.

Pea Soup

    2 pounds green peas, shelled
    3 cups chicken stock
    2 tablespoons crème fraîche or sour cream
    1 tablespoon chopped chives
    salt and pepper to taste

In a large saucepan, cook the peas in the chicken stock until tender (10 to 20 minutes). Season with salt and pepper. Purée in a blender or food processor. Top each serving with a bit of crème fraîche or sour cream and sprinkle with chopped chives.

Yield: 4 servings

Peas with Bibb Lettuce

    6 tablespoons butter
    ½ cup chopped scallions
    8 very small heads of Bibb lettuce, loose outer leaves removed
    3 pounds green peas, shelled
    salt and pepper to taste
    ½ cup chicken stock or water
    1 tablespoon chopped parsley

Melt 4 tablespoons of the butter in a large heavy saucepan. Add the scallions and sauté briefly. Add the peas and lettuce. Sprinkle salt to taste. Add the chicken stock or water, cover, and cook for 20 minutes over low heat until the peas are almost tender. Add the remaining butter, parsley, and pepper. Cook covered for 3 more minutes.
Yield: 4 servings

Pea Salad

    3 ½ cups very young peas, shelled
    2 scallions, chopped
    6 slices bacon, cooked crisp, drained, and crumbled
    1 cup sour cream or plain yogurt
    ⅓ cup mayonnaise
    ½ cup cheddar cheese, grated for topping (optional)
    salt and pepper to taste

Cook the peas until just tender, drain, then chill them for a few hours. Toss the peas with the rest of the ingredients. Top with grated cheddar.
Yield: 6 servings

Peas and Carrots with Pasta

    1 ½ cups bread crumbs
    2 tablespoons olive oil
    ½ cup finely chopped scallions
    2 cups peas, shelled
    1 ½ cups chicken broth
    1 ¼ cups coarsely grated carrots
    ½ cup heavy cream
    1 pound vermicelli, fettucini, fusilli, or rotini
    ½ cup minced fresh mint leaves

Spring

Cook the peas until tender, then drain. In a skillet, cook the bread crumbs in 1 tablespoon oil over moderately low heat, stirring until they are golden brown, then transfer them to a small bowl. In the skillet, cook the scallion in the remaining 1 tablespoon of olive oil over moderately low heat until soft and translucent. Add the peas and the broth, and simmer, stirring, for 3 minutes. Stir in the carrots, simmer the mixture, stirring, for 2 minutes or until the carrots are just tender. Add the cream. Add salt and pepper to taste. Simmer until the liquid is reduced by about one-fourth, remove the sauce from the heat, and keep it warm. Cook the pasta in a kettle of boiling salted water until it is *al dente*, drain, and toss it with the sauce and half the bread crumbs and the mint. Top with remaining bread crumbs and mint.
Yield: 4 servings

Sugar-Snap Peas, Potatoes, and Chives

    1 pound new red potatoes, quartered
    2 tablespoons olive oil
    10 ounces sugar-snap peas, trimmed
    ¼ cup fresh chives

Cook the potatoes in a large pot of boiling water until just tender. Drain. Heat the oil in a large skillet over medium heat. Add the sugar-snap peas and sauté for 2 minutes. Add potatoes and sauté until heated through. Mix in the chives and add salt and pepper to taste.
Yield: 4 servings

Snow Peas and Onion

    ¾ pound snow peas, washed, trimmed, threads removed
    1 large onion
    2 sprigs savory
    salt and pepper to taste

Peel and dice the onion. Boil 1 pint of water, with salt and pepper added to taste. Add the onion and the savory and bring the water to a boil. Add the snow peas and cover the pot. Cook for 25 minutes over medium heat. Check for doneness, then remove snow peas with slotted spoon to a serving dish.
Yield: 6 servings

The Kitchen Gardener's Cookbook

Radishes

Growing Tip: Radishes only take three and a half weeks to grow after sowing. Pull them as soon as you like their size. Radishes grown in the spring taste milder than those grown in hot weather. Black radishes are hot and sharp tasting.

Storing Tip: To keep radishes fresh, trim the leaves and ends and refrigerate in a bowl of cold water.

Sweet and Sour Radishes

    30 radishes with greens attached
    1 teaspoon salt

Marinade:

    1 tablespoon soy sauce
    2 tablespoon rice wine vinegar or distilled vinegar
    1 teaspoon dry sherry
    1 teaspoon sugar
    2 tablespoons Asian sesame oil
    1 tablespoon water

Remove the largest radish leaves. Break the radishes open with the flat side of a large knife. Mix the salt with the radishes, and set aside for 10 minutes. Transfer the radishes to a flat-bottomed bowl. Mix the marinade ingredients together and pour over the radishes. Let stand for 20 minutes or more.

Yield: 3 cups

Radish and Cucumber Salad with Yogurt

    1 cup thinly sliced radishes
    1 cup thinly sliced cucumbers
    1 garlic clove, minced
    1 cup plain yogurt
    2 tablespoons minced fresh mint or parsley leaves

Drain the yogurt in a sieve lined with cheesecloth and set over a bowl (for about 2 hours.) In a bowl, mix the yogurt, cucumbers, radishes, garlic, mint or parsley. Add salt and pepper to taste.

Serve the salad as a side dish on lettuce.

Yield: 4 servings

Spring

Spring Onions and Garlic

Growing Tip: Scallions are mild-flavored and do not form bulbs but divide at the base. They can be planted close together. Leeks also do not form bulbs.

Storing Tip: Sweet onions, which grow in spring and early summer, do not store well because they contain too much moisture. Late-summer and fall onions keep best. You can chop raw onions and store them in bags in the freezer.

Spring Onions with Risotto

    2 tablespoons olive oil
    10 scallions sliced, green and white parts, separated
    1 tablespoon minced garlic
    2 cups sliced leeks, white parts only
    ½ Vidalia or other sweet onion, chopped
    salt and pepper to taste
    2 cups arborio rice
    5 cups chicken stock
    ½ cup dry white wine
    ¼ cup snipped fresh chives
    ¼ cup freshly grated Parmesan

Heat the oil in a large, heavy saucepan over low heat, add the garlic and cook until soft. Add leeks, scallion whites, and onions, raise heat to medium and cook until very soft, 8 to 10 minutes. Season lightly with salt and pepper. Add rice and cook, stirring, 4 to 5 minutes until grains are glossy. In a large saucepan, bring stock to a simmer, add salt to taste. Raise heat under rice to medium high, add wine, and cook, stirring, until liquid is nearly absorbed. Add stock a little at a time until rice is creamy and firm, about 15 to 20 minutes. Stir in chives and half the scallion greens (discard the rest). Cook for 1 minute. Stir in cheese. Serve immediately.
Yield: 4 servings

Onion Tart

Pastry Shell:

    1 cup all-purpose flour
    pinch salt
    ½ cup unsalted butter, cut in small pieces
    3 tablespoons ice water

In a food processor, combine 1 cup flour and pinch of salt. Add 1/2 cup butter. Pulse on/off until mixture resembles coarse meal. While processor is running, gradually add the ice water, processing until dough forms a ball. Shape the dough into a disk. Cover in plastic wrap and refrigerate for 1 hour.

Filling:

    1 ½ pounds onions, sliced

◞ Spring

    2 cloves garlic, finely chopped
    3 tablespoons olive oil
    salt and pepper to taste
    ½ teaspoon chopped fresh thyme
    ½ cup dry white wine
    5 tablespoons unsalted butter
    5 tablespoons flour
    2 cups milk
    4 eggs
    snipped chives

In a large skillet, heat the olive oil and add the onions, garlic, thyme, and salt and pepper to taste. Stir in wine. Cook, stirring often for about 20 to 40 minutes until onions are soft and light amber in color. In a medium saucepan, melt the 5 tablespoons butter, add the 5 tablespoons of flour, and cook, stirring for 2 to 3 minutes until smooth. Gradually stir in the milk. Cook over medium heat, whisking constantly until mixture thickens and boils. Remove from heat. Season to taste with salt and pepper. Whisk several spoonfuls of hot sauce into the eggs until blended. Whisk egg mixture back into hot sauce. Add onion mixture. Mix well.

To assemble:
Preheat the oven to 375 degrees F. Roll out the pastry on a floured surface and fit into a 9-inch pie plate. Trim edge. Pour onion filling into pastry shell spreading evenly to edge. Bake at 375 degrees F for 25 to 30 minutes until custard is just set. Let stand 10 minutes before serving. Garnish with snipped chives. Serve hot or at room temperature.
Yield: 6 servings.

Leek Soup

    6 leeks, white part only
    1 small onion, chopped
    2 tablespoons butter
    3 cups potatoes, peeled and cubed
    6 cups chicken or vegetable stock
    salt and pepper to taste

Cut the leeks into four slices, lengthwise. Wash to remove dirt. Melt the butter in a skillet and sauté the onion and leeks. Add the leeks and onion and the potatoes to the stock. Boil for 25 minutes in a large saucepan until the potatoes are tender. Place in food processor and process until

blended. Return to saucepan and heat. Add more stock if the soup is too thick. Add salt and pepper to taste.
Yield: 6 servings

Sautéed Leeks

    6 leeks
    3 tablespoons butter
    4 teaspoons toasted bread crumbs
    1 teaspoon lemon juice
    salt and pepper to taste

Remove tops and roots of the leeks and wash. Cook the leeks in a pot of boiling water for 10 minutes or until tender. Drain and place in a serving dish. Melt the butter in a skillet and cook until it sizzles and turns golden. Add the bread crumbs, lemon juice, and salt and pepper to taste. When heated, pour the bread crumb mixture over the leeks and serve.
Yield: 4 servings

Garlic Soup

    cloves from 2 heads of garlic, papery skin removed
    6 onions, cut into ½-inch slices
    5 cups chicken broth
    1 ½ teaspoons dried thyme
    4 tablespoons of butter
    1 cup hot milk
    salt and pepper to taste
    6 French-bread slices, cubed

Place the onions and the garlic in a roasting pan, dot with the butter. Add 3 cups of chicken stock. Add thyme and salt and pepper to taste. Cover with aluminum foil. Place in a 350-degree oven and cook for 1½ hours. Turn the garlic and onions. Purée the garlic with the liquid in food processor. Add the remaining 2 cups of chicken stock and milk. Place the soup in a saucepan. Heat the soup. Garnish with bread cubes.
Yield: 6 servings

Roasted Garlic

Preheat oven to 375 degrees F
    1 medium head of garlic

1 tablespoon olive oil

Remove papery outer skin of garlic and, without separating the cloves, put it on a piece of aluminum foil and spoon the olive oil over the garlic. Wrap the garlic in the foil and bake it for 1 hour.

Aioli Sauce

    12 garlic cloves
    3 egg yolks
    14 ounces olive oil
    ½ teaspoon lemon juice

Mash the garlic cloves, add salt and pepper to taste, then add egg yolks, and stir until well blended. Beat in the oil a little at a time. Add the lemon juice.

Asparagus

Growing Tip: Asparagus must be allowed to grow for two full years before it can be harvested. Well-tended asparagus beds push up spears for 6 to 8 weeks each spring. A dozen plants will feed one adult. Asparagus does not keep its flavor after it is picked. Eat your harvest within 24 hours for the best taste.

Freezing Tip: Asparagus freezes well. Scald spears in boiling water for 3 minutes. Chill under cold water, then drain. Store in bags in the freezer.

Parmesan Asparagus

    3 pounds asparagus
    5 tablespoons butter
    2 tablespoons water
    6 ounces grated Parmesan cheese

Cut the ends off the asparagus. Rinse well and drop into boiling salted water and cook until just done. Arrange on a platter. Quickly heat the butter in a small skillet. Add the water and whisk until frothy. Season to taste with salt and pepper. Spoon the butter over the asparagus. Sprinkle the Parmesan cheese on the tips.

Yield: 6 servings

The Kitchen Gardener's Cookbook

Asparagus Bundles

    3 pounds asparagus
    chives cut 6 inches long
    4 tablespoons butter
    2 tablespoons lemon juice

Break ends off asparagus and trim tough part of stalks. Cut stems on diagonal into 4-inch lengths. Cook asparagus in salted boiling water 2 to 3 minutes until tender. Remove asparagus with tongs to a serving platter. When stalks have cooled, tie 4 to 6 stalks with chive length. (Slip a chive blossom into each bundle if possible.) Arrange bundles on the serving plate. Melt butter in a saucepan, whisk in lemon juice. Drizzle over asparagus.

Yield: 6 servings.

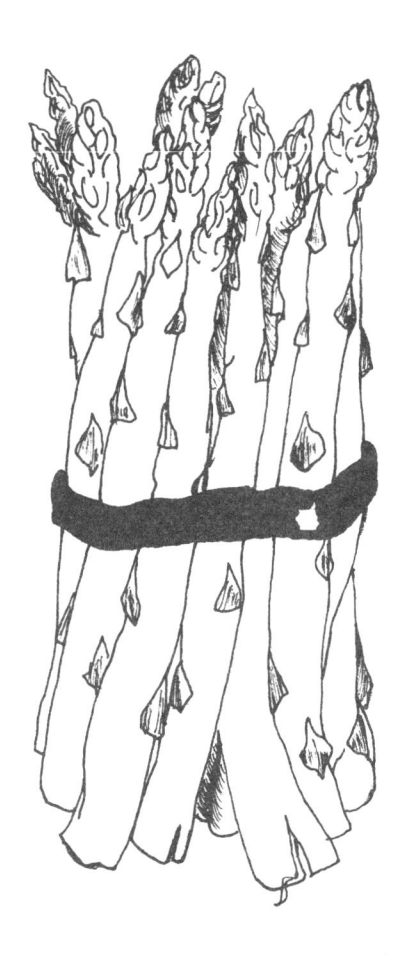

≈ Spring

Risotto Primavera

1 tablespoon olive oil
1 small onion, chopped
4 to 4 ½ cups chicken stock
1 cup arborio rice
½ cup white wine
1 teaspoon dried thyme
¾ pound asparagus
¼ pound sliced carrots
¼ pound plum tomatoes, seeded and chopped
2 ounces Gorgonzola cheese
pepper to taste

Heat the oil in a heavy pot and sauté the onion until soft. Heat the chicken stock almost to boiling. Add the rice to the onion and stir to coat; add the wine and stir. Let the wine cook away (about 2 minutes). Add a cup of the simmering stock to the rice with the thyme. Cook over medium-high heat, stirring often until the mixture has been absorbed. While the risotto is cooking, trim the asparagus by breaking the stems at the point where the tough end meets the tender part. Then cut the asparagus, starting just below the heads, on the diagonal into 1-inch pieces. Continue adding the stock to the rice about a cup at a time, stirring often. Meanwhile, add the carrots to the simmering stock and cook about 7 minutes until they are tender. When the carrots are done, remove them with a slotted spoon and set aside. Add the asparagus to the stock and cook about 3 minutes until just tender; remove and add to the carrots. Continue adding the stock to the rice until it is creamy and tender. Just before you add the last cup of stock, stir in the carrots and asparagus, the tomatoes and Gorgonzola, stirring until the cheese melts. Add salt and pepper to taste.
Yield: 2 servings

Penne with Asparagus and Lemon

2 pounds asparagus
1 ½ teaspoons olive oil
salt and pepper to taste
8 ounces penne
¾ cup chicken stock
2 tablespoons fresh lemon juice

1 ½ teaspoons unsalted butter
1 ounce Parmesan cheese, grated or shaved
4 teaspoons fresh chives
2 tablespoons chopped flat-leaf Italian parsley

Snap or cut off bottoms of asparagus and discard. Cut off tips at an angle and continue to cut stalks into diagonal pieces the same size as the tips. Add asparagus to kettle of boiling water. Cook for 2 to 3 minutes, until the asparagus is tender. Cook penne in a large pot of boiling water until *al dente*. Drain in a colander. Transfer pasta to a large sauté pan. Add chicken stock and lemon juice. Cook over high heat until liquid is almost completely reduced, about 5 minutes. Add butter, three-quarters of the cheese, asparagus, and salt and pepper to taste. Cook, tossing and stirring, until the butter melts. Stir in the herbs. Sprinkle in remaining cheese.
Yield: 4 servings

Parsnips

Parsnip, Garlic, and Potato Purée

2 large baking potatoes, peeled and cut into ½-inch cubes
4 parsnips, peeled and cut into ½-inch-thick rounds
10 cloves roasted garlic, peeled
½ cup low-fat milk
½ stick of butter
salt and pepper to taste

In a large saucepan, combine the potatoes and the parsnips with enough salted cold water to cover. Bring the water to a boil and simmer the vegetables, covered, for 20 to 25 minutes until they are very tender. Drain the vegetables and pass through a ricer into a medium-sized bowl. Stir the roasted garlic and the milk into the purée until well combined. Add the salt and pepper to taste.
Yield: 4 servings

Braised Parsnips

1 pound large parsnips, washed and scraped
3 tablespoons olive oil
½ cup chicken or vegetable broth

◆ Spring

With a vegetable peeler, slice the parsnips into thin slivers. Heat the oil in a skillet, mix in the broth, add the parsnips, and sauté, turning frequently, for 3 minutes. Serve immediately.
Yield: 4 servings

Parsnip and Carrot Purée

    4 parsnips, washed, scraped, and cut in 1/2-inch rounds
    5 carrots, washed, scraped and cut into 4-inch rounds
    1 onion, chopped
    2 tablespoons butter
    1 teaspoon fresh or dried rosemary
    ⅓ cup milk

In a large saucepan, boil the parsnips in enough water to cover, until they are tender. Drain the parsnips. Boil the carrots in enough water to cover, until they are tender. Melt the butter in a skillet and sauté the onion until it is translucent. Purée all the ingredients in a food processor. Add salt and pepper to taste. Transfer to serving dish. Serve hot.
Yield: 4 servings

Beets

Growing Tip: Plant beets before hot weather and thin them carefully to ensure good quality. Harvest them when they are small.

Cooking Tip: Don't peel or cut them until after cooking. Microwaving beets preserves their flavor.

Borscht

    2 to 3 medium beets coarsely grated
    2 small onions, chopped
    2 tablespoons sugar
    1 ½ cups water
    ⅓ cup dry red wine
    2 tablespoons red-wine vinegar
    1 cup cold water
    salt and pepper to taste
    chopped chives
    sour cream or plain yogurt for garnish

Stir the beets, onions, sugar, and 1 ½ cups water in a microwave-safe bowl and microwave the mixture, covered, at high power for 12 to 15 minutes or until the beets are tender. Stir in the wine and microwave at high power for three minutes more. Stir in the cup of cold water, the vinegar, and salt and pepper to taste, transfer the soup to a metal bowl set in a bowl of ice and cold water, and stir until it is cold. Garnish each serving with a dollop of sour cream or yogurt. Sprinkle with chives.
Yield: 6 servings

Beets with Orange and Ginger

6 large beets, cooked until almost tender and cooled
1 medium onion, diced
2 tablespoons butter
1 tablespoon grated fresh ginger
2 tablespoons brown sugar
½ cup orange juice
2 tablespoons raspberry vinegar
½ cup chicken stock
salt and pepper to taste
½ teaspoon cornstarch dissolved in 1 teaspoon water

Peel and slice beets ¼- to ½-inch thick. Melt the butter and sauté the onion until softened, about 2 to 3 minutes. Add ginger, brown sugar, orange juice, vinegar, and chicken stock and combine well. Add beets and cook over low heat for 10 to 15 minutes, stirring frequently. Add salt and pepper to taste. Add dissolved cornstarch and water and cook until just thickened.
Yield: 4 servings

Beet Horseradish

2 medium beets
1 4-ounce piece of fresh horseradish, peeled
¼ cup white wine vinegar
2 teaspoons salt
1 teasoon sugar

Scrub the beets and trim the stems to ½ inch. Place beets in a medium saucepan and add water to cover. Bring to a boil and cook over medium heat at a gentle boil until the beets are tender, about 45 minutes. Remove from the heat, drain, and set aside until cool enough to handle. Grate the horseradish on the medium-size holes of grater box. Mix the

grated horseradish with the vinegar, sugar, and salt. Peel the beets and grate on medium-size holes of box grater. Add to the horseradish and stir well to combine. Cover and refrigerate until needed.
Yield: 1 ½ cups

Pasta with Beets

½ pound cooked, peeled, and diced beets
olive oil
½ pound Gorgonzola or other blue cheese, crumbled
1 cup heavy cream
freshly ground pepper
1 pound fresh egg pasta

If beets are cold, warm them by sautéing them in a little olive oil. Warm the cream and melt half of the cheese in it. Add pepper to taste (usually the cheese has enough salt). Cook the pasta and drain, then toss with the cream mixture. The pasta should be well coated. Add beets and toss, top with remaining cheese.
Yield: 4 servings

Chard

Growing Tip: This type of beet is grown for its leaf and stalk rather than its root. Chard winters over well.

Cooking Tip: Both the leaves and the stalks of chard can be eaten. If leaves are large, however, remove the midribs.

Sautéed Swiss Chard

1 bunch Swiss chard
2 tablespoons olive oil
1 clove garlic, minced
6 scallions thinly sliced
¼ cup chopped fresh basil

Trim the chard, discarding any tough stems. In a large skillet, heat the olive oil, add the garlic and the scallions, and sauté until soft, about 2 to 3 minutes. Add the chard, tossing to coat the leaves. Cover the pan with a lid and heat for 3 to 5 minutes until the chard is wilted and

tender. Add salt and pepper to taste.
Yield: 6 servings

Swiss Chard and Garlic and Penne

    1 pound Swiss chard, stems cut from the leaves, and the stems and leaves chopped separately
    ⅛ teaspoon red-pepper flakes
    1 small onion, chopped fine
    3 large garlic cloves, sliced thin
    2 tablespoons olive oil
    ½ cup water
    ½ cup penne or macaroni
    ¼ cup Parmesan cheese

Rinse and drain the chard leaves and stems separately. In a large heavy skillet, cook the red-pepper flakes, garlic, and onion in the oil over moderate heat, stirring until the garlic is golden. Add the stems and ¼ cup of the water. Cook the mixture, covered, for 5 minutes or until the stems are just tender. Add the leaves with the remaining ¼ cup of water. Add salt and pepper to taste and cook the mixture covered for 3 minutes or until the leaves are tender. While the chard is cooking, boil a kettle of water and cook the penne until it is *al dente*. Drain in a colander. In a large bowl, toss the penne with the chard mixture and add ¼ cup of the Parmesan cheese. Serve with the additional Parmesan.
Yield: 2 servings

Chard Soup

    3 tablespoons olive oil
    1 small yellow onion, minced
    1 teaspoon chopped garlic
    10 medium or 5 large chard leaves, minced
    2 large red potatoes, peeled and cut into ½-inch cubes
    3 cups chicken stock
    3 cups water
    salt and pepper to taste

Heat the olive oil in a heavy stock pot. Add the onion and garlic and sauté for 3 minutes. Add the chard leaves. Add the potatoes, the stock, and the water. Simmer for 45 minutes. Season with salt and pepper.
Yield: 4 servings

Early Summer

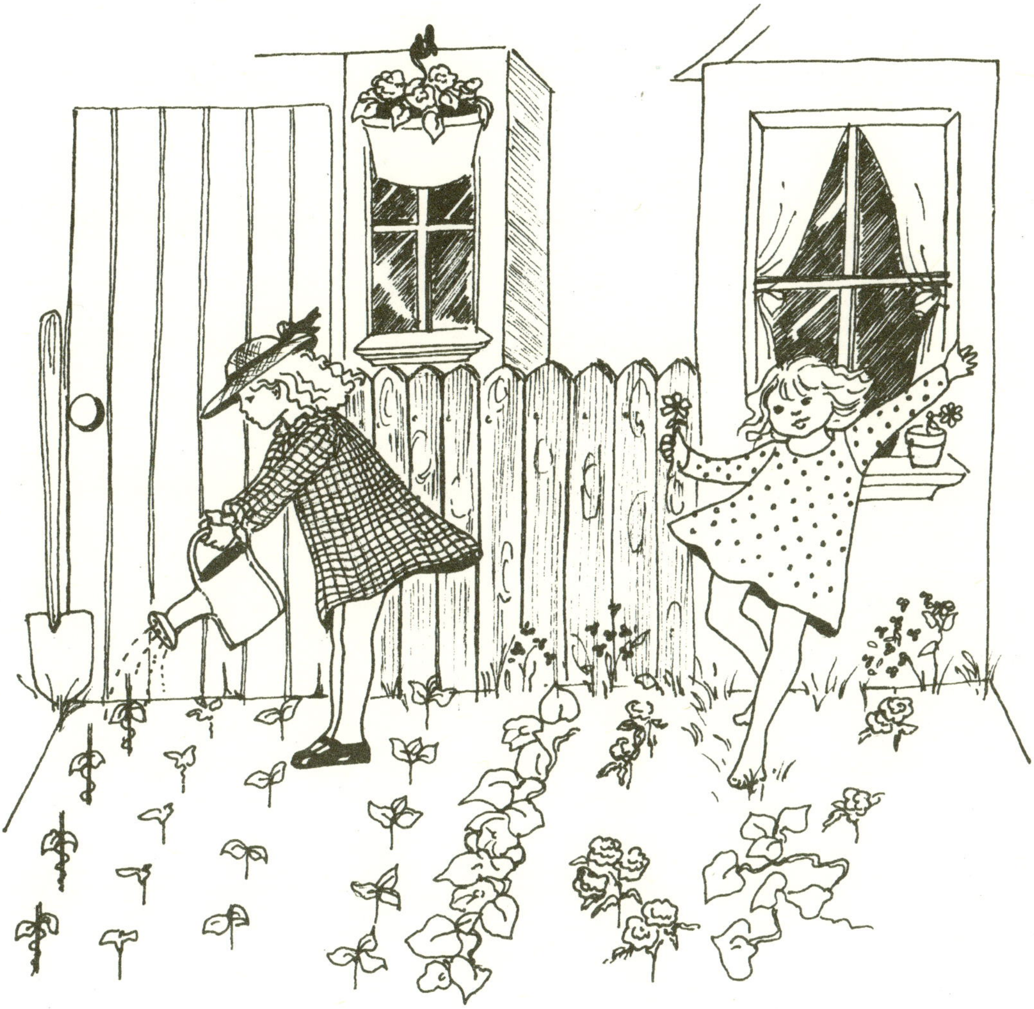

The Kitchen Gardener's Cookbook

◈ **Early Summer**

Before long, our first little house became too small for us. As I planted my garden that spring, after we began looking for a new house, I tried to detach myself from the pleasure it had given me. "Too big," I said as I bent over the rows. "Too much work", I convinced myself, as I turned over the dirt. "In my new house, I'll have a smaller garden," I pretended. The girls' interest in nature was no longer as enthusiastic as it had been when we first moved to the country. They were now five and seven and a little less intrigued by creeping and crawling things. Erin took less delight in plucking slugs off leaves; Lisa spent less time squatting in the dirt looking for night crawlers.

Summer came, and we still hadn't found the house to match our dreams and pocketbook. I signed the girls up for nature camp at the botanical garden in the next town. On the days that I drove the car pool, I passed a house with a For Sale sign on the lawn. It took a couple of weeks of driving by and determining whether or not the house looked and felt like it could belong to us before I called the realtor.

The house had a room for each of us and some to spare, and it was the right price. Outside, there was evidence of a garden, an arrangement of shrubs and lilac bushes. But neglect had brought the wilderness into most of the beds; the ornamental cedars had become tall trees; the shrubs and lilacs all needed pruning and thinning. I found no vestiges of a vegetable garden, but the ideal spot existed for one just outside the kitchen door. We bought the house in the fall and again moved in December. Moving in winter gave us time to work on the house while we waited for spring and the chance to tame and reclaim the garden.

The girls were still interested in having their own vegetable plots. When spring finally came, we tilled the square between the kitchen and the garage and made it into a garden. Each of them got her own area to plant. I tried to assert some influence over how many rows of peas to sow and how far apart to plant the cherry tomatoes. Erin was meticulous in her garden care. She weeded and watered and thinned. Lisa was more casual, which didn't affect production. Her little plot yielded as much as her sister's. Erin did not approve of her sister's gardening ethic nor did she tolerate the idea of sharing her produce. Lisa would have given away her entire harvest. Even at an early age, Erin wanted to experiment with unusual vegetables — she had done zucchini; she was ready for eggplant and pear tomatoes. Lisa grew what she liked to eat, and as her palate was limited to peanut-butter-and-jelly sandwiches, she had to be convinced to plant tomatoes and peas. She liked to grow flowers: big suns of marigolds, sweet-faced pansies. The johnny jump-ups she planted by the fence still come up each year.

When I recall my daughters' early gardening techniques, I realize how clearly they represent the way they still conduct their lives. Lisa is carefree and relaxed. She finds contentment in a bowl of fat raspberries or a sliced tomato when she visits. Erin is meticulous and orderly. She loves innovation and change. "Why don't you try planting golden raspberries or baby patty-pan squash," she'll suggest as we stroll around the yard. I still see them on a hot July morning, picking raspberries in a friend's enormous garden. Lisa was a one-for-the-mouth, one-for-the-bucket picker. Erin would count each berry as it dropped from her hand into her plastic container. When it was time to go home, Erin had more than Lisa, and it was difficult to settle the ensuing battle. Lisa could not accept the abstract notion that berries eaten counted as berries picked. And her sister was not about to share what she had so diligently accrued. While they might not agree that berry-picking is a defining metaphor for their lives, they don't dispute that it sweetens memory: the first burst of juice on the tongue, red-stained fingers, berries glinting in their buckets.

Green Beans

Growing Tip: Although seed companies have worked hard to develop beans without strings, some of the most flavorful beans have them. Don't be afraid to plant some.

Cooking Tip: Green beans require a minimum of cooking.

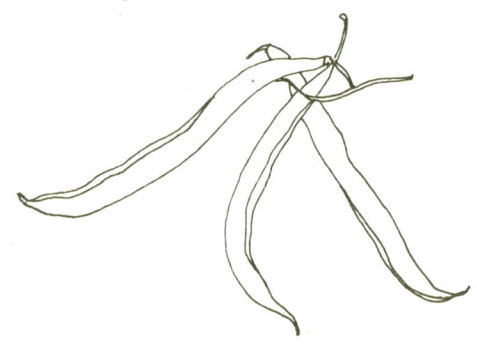

🍃 Early Summer

Steamed Green Beans

¾ pound thin green beans, trimmed

In a steamer set over a saucepan of boiling water, steam the beans, covered for 3 to 6 minutes, or until they are just tender.
Salt and pepper to taste. The beans can be steamed in a microwave also.
Yield: 6 servings

Green Beans, Garlic, and Almonds

2 pounds early green beans, trimmed
1 large bulb garlic, roasted (see garlic recipes)
½ cup almond slivers
¼ cup olive oil
2 tablespoons red-wine vinegar

Steam the beans or blanch until just tender. Cool by plunging them into cold water. Drain and set aside. Squeeze the roasted garlic pulp from the garlic cloves. Combine the roasted garlic pulp with the almonds, the olive oil, and the vinegar and mix together. Toss with the drained beans and allow to sit at room temperature for an hour before serving.
Yield: 6 servings

Green Beans with Ginger

1 pound early green beans, trimmed and cut into ½-inch pieces
1 tablespoon butter
1 small onion, thinly sliced
2 teaspoons finely chopped fresh ginger
¼ cup chicken stock

salt and pepper to taste

Heat butter in a large skillet. Add the onion, ginger, and salt and pepper to taste. Sauté until the onions are translucent. Add the beans and the chicken stock. Cover and cook until the beans are just tender.
Yield: 4 servings

Green-Bean Pâté

½ pound fresh green beans
1 tablespoon olive oil
1 onion, chopped

3 hard-cooked eggs
1 tablespoon lemon juice
3 tablespoons chopped parsley leaves
salt and pepper to taste

Cook the beans until just tender by boiling or steaming them. In a skillet, heat the oil; add the onion and sauté until softened. Cool. Put green beans, onion, eggs, parsley, and lemon juice in food processor and pulse until puréed. Add salt and pepper to taste. Chill. Serve with crackers.
Yield: 2 cups

Marinated String Beans

1 pound string beans, trimmed

Marinade:

1 garlic clove, chopped
2 scallions, cut into 2-inch lengths
½ cup virgin olive oil
⅓ cup red-wine vinegar
1 tablespoon chopped fresh thyme or 1 teaspoon dried thyme
salt and pepper to taste

Steam the beans for 5 minutes or until just tender. Allow to cool. Combine the marinade ingredients. Toss the beans with the marinade. Cover and refrigerate at least 3 hours.
Yield: 4 servings

Green-Bean and Radish Salad

1 pound green beans, trimmed and cut into 2-inch lengths
3 tablespoons olive oil
1 tablespoon white vinegar
½ teaspoon dried tarragon
1 cup diced red radishes
1 scallion, sliced thin
salt and pepper to taste

Bring a large saucepan of water to boil, add the green beans, and cook until tender, about 4 minutes. Drain under cold running water, transfer to serving bowl. In a small bowl, whisk the oil, vinegar, tarragon, and salt and pepper to taste. Add the dressing and the radishes to the beans and toss well. Sprinkle with the scallion.
Yield: 6 servings

▧ Early Summer

Green-Bean Vinaigrette with Red Onion and Dill

    1 medium red onion, chopped fine
    1 pound green beans, trimmed and cut in half
    2 tablespoons red wine vinegar
    salt and pepper to taste
    ½ teaspoon dry mustard
    ¼ cup olive oil
    1 tablespoon chopped dill

Place the onion in a large bowl. In a steamer set over boiling water, steam the green beans, covered, for 5 to 6 minutes until just tender and add them to the onions. In a small bowl, whisk the vinegar with the salt and pepper and mustard. Add the oil in a slow stream until the dressing is combined. Pour the dressing over the beans with the dill and mix well.
Yield: 4 servings

The Kitchen Gardener's Cookbook

Green-Bean and Fingerling-Potato Salad

    1 pound white or purple fingerling potatoes. (If fingerling potatoes are not available, small red potatoes, halved, may be substituted.)
    ½ pound green beans, trimmed
    ⅛ cup mixed fresh herbs
    1 tablespoon olive oil
    salt and pepper to taste

In a large kettle of enough salted water to just cover them, simmer the potatoes about 10 minutes or until tender and drain them in a colander. In a large saucepan, cook the beans in 3 inches of boiling water until tender, about 3 to 5 minutes. Transfer the beans to the colander with the potatoes and drain well. In a large bowl, toss together the potatoes, the beans, herbs, oil, and salt and pepper to taste.
Yield: 6 servings

Green-Bean, Yellow-Pepper, and Bacon Salad

    1 pound green beans, trimmed
    1 tablespoon red-wine vinegar
    1 teaspoon Dijon-style mustard
    ½ teaspoon dried oregano, crumbled
    ¼ cup olive oil
    1 small yellow pepper, cut into thin strips
    6 slices lean bacon, cooked until crisp and drained

In a kettle of boiling water, cook the beans for 2 to 4 minutes until they are tender. Drain and cool them under cold running water. In a large bowl, whisk together the vinegar, mustard, oregano; add the oil in a stream. Add the beans, yellow pepper, and the bacon, crumbled. Add salt and pepper to taste.
Yield: 6 servings

Broccoli

Growing Tip: Broccoli comes right after the first pea harvest. It can survive frost and snow and will keep producing after being cut. Harvest broccoli when the florets are small and firm. Cut the stalks at an angle.

Cooking Tip: Broccoli and cauliflower can be exchanged in most recipes.

Early Summer

Broccoli freezes well. Blanch the broccoli and drain, then place in bags and freeze.

Spiced Broccoli
    1 large bunch broccoli
    ¼ cup olive oil
    1 large garlic clove, minced
    ¼ teaspoon red-pepper flakes

Steam the broccoli until tender. Heat the olive oil in a skillet, add the garlic and red-pepper flakes. Drain the broccoli and transfer to serving platter. Drizzle the garlic-pepper oil over it.
Yield: 4 servings

Broccoli Stir-fry
    ½ pound broccoli florets, cut into 4-inch thin strips
    3 tablespoons peanut oil
    2 teaspoons minced garlic
    2 teaspoons fresh ginger
    1 tablespoon dark soy sauce
    1 tablespoon cornstarch dissolved in 2 tablespoons of water

Heat the peanut oil in a wok or large skillet. Add the garlic and the ginger and cook for 30 seconds, stirring constantly. Add the soy sauce and the broccoli, stir-fry for 2 to 3 minutes. Add the cornstarch to the mixture and stir until it thickens. This is easily adapted to include other ingredients — add chicken or shrimp and other vegetables to skillet and cook for requisite amount of time.

Broccoli Salad
    2 heads of broccoli, cut into medium florets with 1-inch stems

Parsley and Red-Pepper Dressing:
    ¼ cup olive oil
    2 tablespoons chopped parsley
    2 tablespoons chopped red pepper
    2 tablespoons white-wine vinegar
    1 tablespoon chopped chives
    1 tablespoon chopped tarragon
    salt and pepper to taste

½ clove of garlic, minced

Whisk together all the dressing ingredients. Let sit so flavors will blend. Boil a pot of water and cook the broccoli until tender. (The broccoli can also be steamed.) Transfer to a bowl of ice water to keep broccoli bright. Drain and refrigerate until well cooled. Arrange the broccoli on a serving platter and pour dressing over it.

Yield: 4 to 6 servings

Broccoli Soup

1 head of broccoli, chopped
1 medium baking potato, chopped
1 small onion, chopped
5 cups chicken broth (vegetable bouillon can be substituted)
2 garlic cloves
1 teaspoon curry powder

Simmer the stock, broccoli, potato, onion and garlic cloves for 20 minutes or until the vegetables are very tender. Add the curry powder and simmer for another 5 minutes. Transfer the vegetables with a little of the stock to a blender and purée. If you like a creamy soup, you can add 1 cup plain nonfat yogurt. Return to the pot and mix with the remaining stock.

Yield: 4 servings

Broccoli Lemon Risotto

4 cups chicken broth
2 cups water
1 pound broccoli, cut into florets, stems cut into ½-inch cubes
1 teaspoon grated lemon zest
1 tablespoon fresh lemon juice
1 small onion, chopped fine
1 garlic clove, minced
2 tablespoons olive oil
1 ½ cups arborio rice
½ cup grated Parmesan cheese

Bring the broth and the water to a boil in a large saucepan and simmer the broccoli florets for 3 minutes or until they are tender. Transfer the florets to a bowl and reserve them. Add the broccoli stems, the lemon zest, and the lemon juice to the broth and simmer for 5 minutes. While

Early Summer

the stems are cooking, sauté the onion and garlic in the oil over moderately low heat, add the rice, and turn until each grain is coated with the oil. Add ½ cup of the broth with cooked stems and cook the mixture, stirring constantly, until the broth is absorbed. Continue adding broth mixture, ½ cup at a time, stirring and letting each portion be absorbed until adding the next, until rice is *al dente*. Rice should cook about 20 minutes. Stir in reserved broccoli florets and simmer the risotto, stirring, until florets are heated through. Remove the pan from the heat and stir in the Parmesan. Add salt and pepper to taste.
Yield: 2 servings

Carrots

Growing Tip: Harvest carrots when they are small for the best flavor. You can harvest carrots after a frost. Sometimes, carrots are sweeter if they have been frozen.

Cooking Tip: You don't need to peel summer carrots, just scrub them with a soft brush under running water. Place carrots, patted dry, in plastic bags to store. Some varieties will keep in a crisper until next spring. Carrots are wonderful when combined with herbs or spices such as mint, cinnamon, or ginger and sautéed in a butter or olive oil.

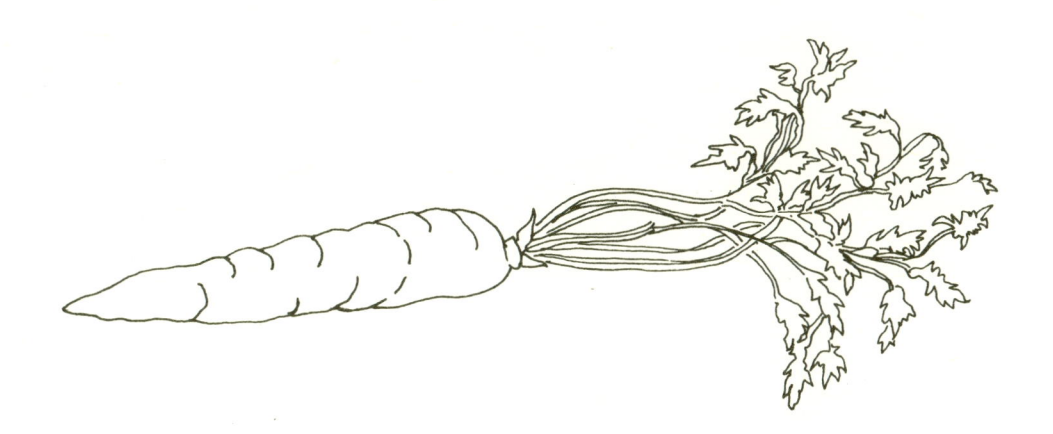

Lemon Carrots with Dill

    1 pound carrots, cut into ½-inch slices
    1 to 2 tablespoons lemon juices
    2 tablespoons fresh dill

Steam the carrots for about 7 minutes until tender. Drain. Add the dill and lemon juice.
Yield: 4 servings

Carrot Salad

    4 cups shredded carrots
    1 cup raisins (optional)
    ½ cup cider vinegar
    ¼ cup salad oil
    ½ teaspoon celery seeds
    ½ teaspoon dry mustard
    ⅓ cup sugar
    2 tablespoons parsley, chopped fine

Mix together carrots, raisins, and parsley. Combine vinegar, oil, celery seeds, mustard, and sugar in a saucepan and bring to a boil. Pour over carrot mixture and chill until ready to serve.
Yield: 6 servings

Carrots with Brown Sugar

    1 ½ pounds baby carrots, peeled
    3 tablespoons butter
    2 tablespoons dark-brown sugar
    1 clove garlic, minced (optional)

Cook the carrots in a saucepan in ½ cup of water until just tender, 8 to 10 minutes. Drain and set aside. Melt the butter with the brown sugar in the same saucepan. Return the carrots to the pan and toss with the sugar mixture for a few minutes until caramelized.
Yield: 6 servings

Ginger Carrots

    2 pounds baby carrots, scrubbed
    3 tablespoons butter
    2 tablespoons chopped fresh ginger

    1 teaspoon fresh dill
    1 large garlic clove, minced
    1 ½ tablespoons brown sugar

Steam the carrots until tender. In a saucepan, melt the butter, add the brown sugar and garlic, ginger and dill, then add the drained carrots and sauté 2 to 3 minutes.

Yield: 6 servings

Carrot Cake

    1 cup butter, room temperature
    2 cups sugar
    3 eggs
    2 ½ cups flour
    2 teaspoons baking soda
    1 tablespoon salt
    1 teaspoon cinnamon
    ½ teaspoon nutmeg
    1 tablespoon vanilla
    2 cups carrots, shredded

Cream the butter and sugar until light and fluffy. Add the eggs one at a time. In a large bowl, mix sifted dry ingredients. Fold in grated carrots and pour batter into 10-inch greased tube pan. Bake in a 350-degree oven for 45 to 50 minutes.

Cream-Cheese Frosting:

    8 ounces cream cheese, room temperature
    1 box confectioners' sugar
    12 tablespoons (1 ½ sticks) butter

Cream together the cream cheese, sugar, and butter. Frost the cake when it has cooled.

Carrot Soup

    3 cups chicken or vegetable stock
    1 small onion, chopped
    5 carrots, peeled and sliced
    ⅛ teaspoon nutmeg
    1 tablespoon Worcestershire sauce
    1 clove garlic, minced

¼ cup orange juice
salt and pepper to taste

Simmer all the ingredients in the stock about 15 minutes or until tender. Purée and reheat before serving.

Yield: 4 servings

Eggplant

Growing Tip: Harvest eggplant when small for best flavor and texture. Asian eggplant ripens earlier than other varieties.

Cooking Tip: Do not cook eggplant in aluminum pans. Using a sterling-silver spoon to scoop out eggplant flesh when required will prevent discoloring. When microwaving eggplant, prick several times on both sides with a fork to prevent bursting.

Eggplant Salad

1 eggplant, 9 to 10 ounces
½ pound zucchini
1 tablespoon olive oil
2 tablespoons coriander leaves
1 tablespoon lemon juice
1 ½ teaspoons mint
1 tablespoon parsley, chopped

Cut the eggplant into ½-inch-thick slices and then into cubes. Cut the zucchini into pieces of the same size. Heat a skillet and add ½ tablespoon of the olive oil and sauté the zucchini for three minutes; transfer to serving dish. Add another ½ tablespoon of olive oil to the pan and sauté the eggplant pieces. Sauté for three minutes until tender. Add the eggplant to the zucchini and add salt and pepper to taste; add the lemon juice and herbs. Toss to mix well.

Yield: 4 servings

Grilled Eggplant

6 small Japanese eggplants
½ cup olive oil
salt and pepper to taste

Cut the eggplants in half along the stem (vertically). Brush with olive oil and season with salt and pepper. Grill for a few minutes on each side until tender.
Yield: 6 servings

Baba Ghanouj

    2 medium-sized eggplants (1 to 1 ¼ pounds each)
    ¼ cup olive oil
    2 tablespoons lemon juice
    2 teaspoons minced garlic cloves
    1 green chili pepper, chopped
    a handful of parsley (long stems removed)

Roast the eggplants on a baking sheet in a 400-degree oven until they burst and the centers become tender, about 1 ½ hours. For quicker cooking, pierce the eggplants with a fork and place on paper towel and cook in microwave on high for 15 minutes or until soft inside. Open each eggplant immediately and scoop out pulp onto the baking sheet. When cool, place eggplant pulp in food processor with other ingredients and purée until coarsely blended. Cover and chill until ready to serve. Serve with pita triangles or crackers.
Yield: 3 cups

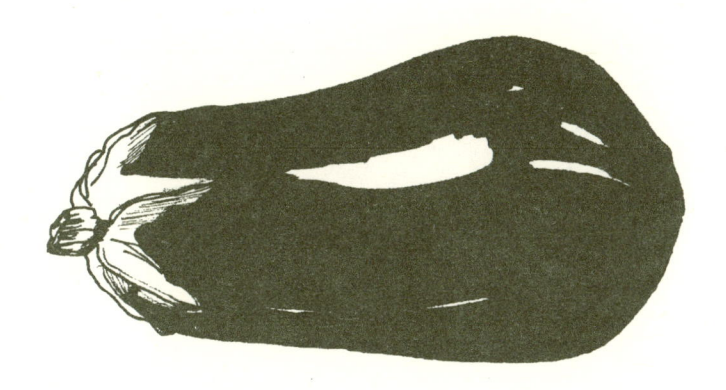

Ratatouille

    ¼ cup olive oil
    2 medium eggplants, cut in ½-inch slices, then into wedges
    6 zucchini, peeled and sliced into ½-inch rounds
    4 tomatoes, chopped
    2 onions, coarsely chopped
    2 cloves garlic, minced
    2 green peppers, chopped
    salt and pepper to taste
    ¼ teaspoon oregano
    2 fresh basil leaves, chopped

Sauté the onion and garlic in 2 tablespoons of olive oil in a large skillet or Dutch oven until soft. Add the rest of the oil and cook the eggplants and zucchini for five minutes, stirring frequently. Add the tomatoes, peppers, oregano, and basil. Add salt and pepper to taste and simmer over low heat for 45 minutes. Stir often.

Yield: 6 servings

Eggplant Parmesan

    2 medium eggplants
    ¼ cup flour
    olive oil
    2 cloves garlic, minced
    6 tomatoes, peeled and chopped
    1 tablespoon Italian parsley, minced
    1 tablespoon basil, chopped
    1 teaspoon thyme
    1 onion, chopped
    salt and pepper to taste
    ½ cup red wine
    ½ cup grated Parmesan cheese
    1 pound mozzarella cheese, thinly sliced

Slice the eggplants into ½-inch rounds. Coat each round with flour and fry in oil until soft. Transfer the eggplant slices to paper towel. Cook the garlic, tomatoes, onion, parsley, thyme, and basil in the olive oil for about 30 minutes. Add the red wine and simmer until the sauce thickens. In a greased baking dish, layer the eggplant, then the sauce, then the cheeses on top. Bake 30 to 40 minutes at 350 degrees.

🍂 Early Summer

Caponata

1 large eggplant, peeled and cut into ½-inch cubes
¼ cup olive oil
4 tomatoes, peeled, seeded and cut into ½-inch cubes
1 green pepper, seeded and chopped
2 cloves garlic, minced
1 sweet onion, chopped
¼ cup capers, drained
2 tablespoons parsley, minced
2 tablespoons red-wine vinegar
8 pitted green or black olives
salt and pepper to taste

Heat the olive oil in a large skillet with a cover. Add the eggplant and cook, covered, about 15 minutes until very soft. Add the tomatoes and cook 3 minutes. Transfer the eggplant-tomato mixture to a large bowl and let cool. Add the green pepper, onion, garlic, capers, parsley, vinegar; add salt and pepper to taste. Chop the olives and add them to the mixture. Chill the caponata until ready to serve.
Yield: 4 servings

Cauliflower

Growing Tip: Harvest the cauliflower when the head is 6 to 8 inches in diameter. Cut the head where it meets the stem.

Cooking Tip: Trim a medium-sized cauliflower and place it in a brown-paper bag. Wet the bag under cold running water, then prick the bag with a sharp knife several times. Fold over the top of the bag and microwave on full power for 10 minutes.

Cauliflower in Bread Crumbs

2 cups cauliflower florets
½ cup bread crumbs
3 tablespoons butter

Melt the butter in a skillet, add the bread crumbs and cook until browned. Meanwhile, microwave, steam, or boil cauliflower until soft. Small florets can be sautéed in butter before adding the bread crumbs.

Transfer to serving dish. Cover with browned bread crumbs.
Yield: 4 servings

Cauliflower Soup

    1 head cauliflower, cut into florets
    2 cups chicken or vegetable broth
    3 tablespoons butter
    3 tablespoons flour
    1 ½ cups milk
    1 tablespoon chopped parsley
    salt and pepper to taste

Cook the cauliflower in the broth until just tender. Remove the cauliflower from the broth and place in food processor with 1 cup of the broth. Blend until puréed; return to the pot. Melt the butter in a skillet and stir in the flour, stirring for several minutes; add to the purée and mix well. Add the milk. Add salt and pepper to taste. Stir the soup until thickened. Add the chopped parsley for garnish.
Yield: 4 servings

Cauliflower Salad

    1 head cauliflower, cut into florets
    1 red pepper, chopped
    2 tablespoons parsley, chopped
    3 scallions, white part, sliced thin; green part, chopped
    1 small zucchini, unpeeled, sliced and chopped

Mix all the ingredients in a salad bowl.

Garlic Dressing:

    1 garlic clove, minced
    2 tablespoons red-wine vinegar or lemon juice
    ½ teaspoon dry mustard
    5 tablespoons olive oil
    salt and pepper to taste

Combine the ingredients in a bowl and mix well. Pour over salad and toss.
Yield: 4 to 6 servings

🌿 **Early Summer**

Cauliflower and Cheese

    1 cauliflower, cut into florets
    ¼ cup butter, cut in slices
    ½ pound mild cheddar cheese, sliced
    salt and pepper to taste

Boil, steam, or microwave cauliflower until tender. Drain and place in baking dish. Dot with butter and cover with cheddar cheese. Sprinkle on salt and pepper to taste. Bake in 350-degree oven until cheese has melted and is bubbling.

Yield: 4 servings

Greens

Growing Tip: Lettuces grow quickly so don't plant more than you can eat regularly. For 4 servings, you need to harvest 4 to 5 cups greens. Cut stems about 1 inch above the soil with scissors when the greens are about 5 inches long. Fertilize greens once a week with fish emulsion. You should get 3 to 4 harvests a season.

Cooking Tip: Mesclun is a mix of tender greens, young lettuces, and herbs. Greens are delicious when slightly wilted in a little olive oil. Spray lettuce with water from a spray bottle before storing in plastic bags in the refrigerator. Lettuce leaves should be torn, not chopped with a knife.

Lettuce Salad with Raspberry Dressing

    2 small heads of Bibb or Buttercrunch lettuce
    1 small head red leaf lettuce
    ½ cup toasted walnuts

Tear lettuce and place in serving bowl. Garnish with walnuts.

Raspberry Dressing:

    ¼ cup fresh raspberries
    1 tablespoon sugar
    3 tablespoons raspberry vinegar
    1 teaspoon mustard
    1 tablespoon plain yogurt

⅓ cup olive oil

In a food processor, combine ¼ cup raspberries, sugar, raspberry vinegar, mustard, and yogurt. Add oil in a thin stream until blended. Cover and refrigerate until ready to serve, then spoon dressing over salad.
Yield: 4 to 6 servings

Mesclun Salad

    8 cups mixed baby greens, washed and dried
    2 ½ tablespoons olive oil
    2 teaspoons sherry vinegar
    salt and pepper to taste

Toss the mesclun in a salad bowl with the olive oil. Drizzle it with the vinegar. Add salt and pepper to taste. Toss well.
Yield: 6 servings

Arugula and Basil Salad

    2 teaspoons balsamic vinegar
    2 tablespoons olive oil
    1 ½ tablespoons vegetable oil
    2 small bunches of arugula, stems removed
    12 fresh basil leaves
    2 ounces Parmesan cheese, thinly shaved

In a large bowl, whisk the vinegar and salt and pepper. Whisk in the olive oil and vegetable oil. Add the arugula and basil and toss to combine. Spoon the salad onto plates and top with Parmesan cheese shavings.
Yield: 4 servings

Endive Salad

    1 head curly endive, torn into bite-sized pieces
    1 cup sliced cucumber, peeled
    1 small sweet onion, sliced and separated into rings
    ½ pound feta cheese, crumbled
    18 black olives

Lemon and Oregano Dressing:
    ¼ cup fresh lemon juice
    ¾ cup olive oil
    3 teaspoons fresh oregano

Layer the endive and cucumber and onion, then olives and cheese. Cover and refrigerate to chill. Whisk together the dressing ingredients and pour about ½ cup of the mixture over the salad. Toss lightly.
Yield: 6 servings

Garden Salad

    2 heads radicchio
    2 heads mâche (lamb's lettuce)
    4 sorrel leaves
    12 to 14 arugula leaves
    ¾ cup basil (red, green, or mixed) leaves

Wash and dry salad greens and tear all but 6 radicchio leaves into bite-sized pieces and combine with basil leaves in salad bowl. Line the sides of the bowl with the radicchio leaves.

Parsley and Chive Dressing:

    2 scallions, chopped fine
    1 teaspoon Dijon mustard
    2 tablespoons lemon juice
    1 tablespoon minced parsley
    1 tablespoon chopped chives
    salt and pepper to taste
    ¾ cup olive oil

Combine all the ingredients except the oil. Add the oil in a thin stream and whisk until blended. Add salt and pepper to taste. Refrigerate until ready to use.
Yield: 4 to 6 servings

Caesar Salad

    1 large head Romaine lettuce
    2 cups French-bread cubes
    ½ cup Parmesan cheese
    ¾ cup olive oil
    juice of one lemon
    3 garlic cloves
    1 teaspoon Worcestershire sauce
    1 teaspoon Dijon mustard
    salt and pepper to taste

Wash and dry Romaine and tear into bite-sized pieces. In a food processor, mince 3 garlic cloves, 2 tablespoons of the Parmesan, lemon juice, Worcestershire, oil, and mustard and blend. Transfer to a bowl and season with salt and pepper. Add to Romaine. Add croutons, toss and mix with the rest of the Parmesan cheese.
Yield: 4 servings

Green Salad and Goat-Cheese Toasts

    4 cups curly chicory
    2 cups arugula
    1 tablespoon red-wine vinegar
    1 teaspoon Dijon mustard
    ¾ cup olive oil
    salt and pepper to taste
    12 ⅓-inch-thick slices of French bread
    3 tablespoons olive oil
    2 ounces mild goat cheese

Wash and dry the chicory and arugula. Whisk together the vinegar and mustard; add salt and pepper to taste. Add the oil in a stream and blend thoroughly. Toss with the greens. Mix with the additional herb dressing listed below. Toast the bread on a rack under preheated broiler, turning once, until it is golden, then brush with 2 ½ teaspoons of the olive oil. In a small bowl, mix the goat cheese with the remaining ½ teaspoon oil and spread the mixture on the toasts. Broil the toasts on the rack under broiler for 1 minute or until cheese is slightly browned. Serve two cheese toasts with each portion of salad.
Yield: 6 servings

Herb Dressing:
    1 tablespoon white-wine vinegar
    1 tablespoon parsley, minced
    ¼ teaspoon thyme, crumbled
    ¼ teaspoon dried basil, crumbled

Red and Green Salad

    1 small head red leaf lettuce
    1 small head Bibb lettuce
    ½ cup thinly sliced scallion

◈ Early Summer

    2 tablespoons white-wine vinegar
    ⅓ cup olive oil

Wash and dry the lettuces and toss in a bowl with the scallion. Whisk together the vinegar and salt and pepper to taste, add the oil in a thin stream until blended. Toss the salad with the dressing.
Yield: 6 servings

Romaine and Chicory Salad

    1 head Romaine lettuce
    1 head chicory
    1 ½ cups toasted French-bread cubes (croutons)
    ⅓ cup olive oil
    juice from ½ large lemon
    1 cup parsley, stems removed
    ¼ cup Parmesan cheese
    salt and pepper to taste

Wash and dry lettuce and chicory and toss in a bowl with the croutons. In a food processor, blend the oil, lemon juice, parsley, and Parmesan. Add salt and pepper to taste. Pour over salad and toss.
Yield: 4 servings

Mixed Greens with Poppy-Seed Dressing

    2 cups arugula
    1 small head curly chicory
    1 small head Boston lettuce

Wash and dry greens. Tear into bite-sized pieces and toss in a bowl.

Poppy-Seed Dressing:

    1 egg
    ½ cup sugar
    1 tablespoon Dijon-style mustard
    ⅔ cup red-wine vinegar
    2 cups corn oil
    3 tablespoons poppy seeds

In a food processor, blend the egg, sugar, mustard, and vinegar. With the motor running, pour in the oil in a slow stream. When well blended, transfer to a bowl and stir in the poppy seeds. Add salt to taste.

The Kitchen Gardener's Cookbook

Watercress and Scallion Salad

    2 pounds watercress, stemmed and chopped
    4 scallions, sliced into ¼-inch rounds
    2 teaspoons light soy sauce
    2 tablespoons Asian sesame oil
    1 ½ teaspoons sugar
    salt and pepper to taste

Toss the watercress and scallions in a bowl. Mix together the soy sauce, olive oil, and sugar, and add salt and pepper to taste.

Yield: 4 servings

Summer

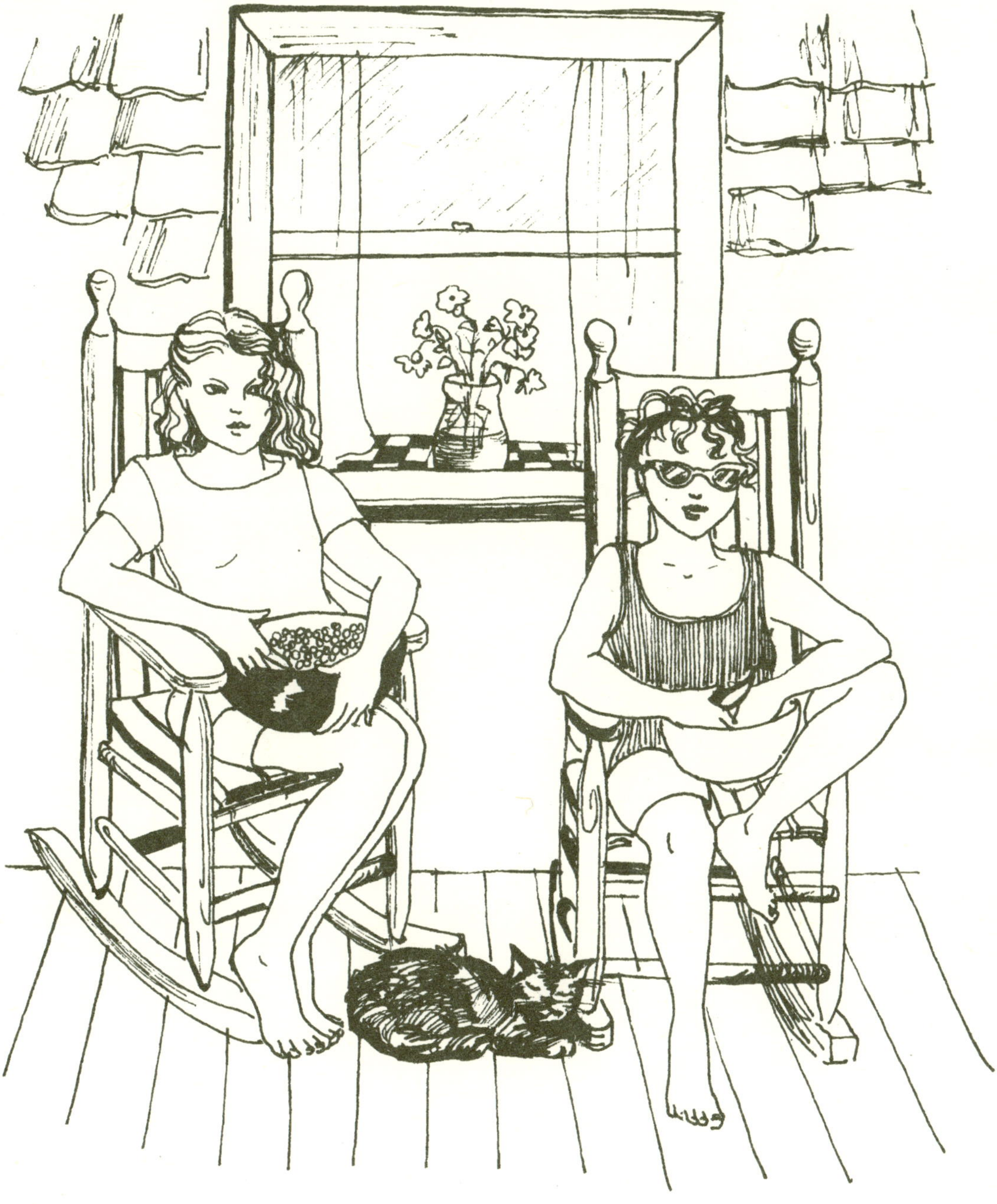

The Kitchen Gardener's Cookbook

Summer

Every summer, we rent a house on an island in Maine for a week or two. As much as I look forward to time away, to sailing and beachcombing and lobster picnics on the beach, to falling alseep to the sound of the lighthouse bell and distant fog-horn, to visits with summer friends, I hate to leave my garden. A week or two away and the lettuce can bolt, the tomatoes ripen, the mint find new places to set up permanent camp. I miss being witness to the next crop of greens and peas uncurling from the dirt.

Luckily, the house we rent comes with a vegetable garden. The patch dug into the slope behind the old sea-captain's house holds carrots, beans, peas, potatoes, onions, lettuce, tomatoes, and squash and enough herbs to season a seafood dinner or pasta salad. The garden thrives on seaweed fertilizer and foggy mornings. Each spring, the owner calls a local teenager and asks him to rototill the garden so she can plant it when she comes to Maine. When she arrives on Memorial Day weekend, invariably, the garden has not been tilled, so she does it herself, carefully calculating and plotting her rows and determining where to sow and plant her seeds and plants. When she returns to stay for the months of June and July, she discovers the teenage boy remembered his job and has tilled the garden. Everything she planted in orderly rows comes up, but in an entirely different location.

When we rent the house later in the summer, the garden has reached its peak and we reap the benefits. Cascading nasturtiums drape the garden wall. The kitchen table, covered with a blue and white checked cloth, always holds a milk jug or mayonnaise jar of red and orange and yellow blooms. My daughters loved this garden when they were young and took on its care and picked its produce without complaint. They'd sit on the old rockers on the porch shelling peas for dinner. Everything from the garden, infused with ocean air and sunshine and the pleasure of vacation, tasted delicious.

At the end of our stay, bags of lettuce and tomatoes and zucchini, a stray kitten found on the beach, buckets of shells and stones smoothed and rounded by the ocean's pounding, and enough sand to keep me sweeping and shaking out towels for weeks to come, accompanied us on the long car ride home. We combined our Maine vegetables with the ones from our garden, comparing the difference, savoring the mix of flavors and places.

When the girls reached adolescence, vacations on islands in Maine, like many things, lost their allure. Their summers were spent traveling or working. Their schedules did not include time for gardens, for shelling peas or digging carrots, or for the long drive to Maine. As they moved toward separating from us and from their childhood, I missed them more than I do now when they no longer live at home. I knew they needed at this time to be different and distant and disapproving, just as I guessed they would eventually return to what they had first cared about: nature and bugs and shelling peas and islands in Maine.

Cucumbers

Growing Tip: There are two categories of cucumbers: slicing and pickling. Because cucumbers have shallow roots, they need consistent watering. Cucumbers grow quickly, so pick them every few days.

Cooking Tip: Burpless cucumbers are more tender than those with seeds. Small, young cucumbers have fewer seeds than more mature cucumbers. Cucumbers are usually eaten raw.

Dilled Cucumbers

    3 large cucumbers, peeled and sliced very thin
    salt
    ⅔ cup white-wine vinegar
    ½ cup water
    ½ cup sugar
    ½ teaspoon white pepper
    salt to taste
    2 tablespoons chopped fresh dill

Arrange cucumbers in layers, and sprinkle each layer with salt. Cover with wax paper and put heavy skillet (or similar heavy weight) on top. Leave at room temperature for several hours and drain them thoroughly. Boil vinegar, sugar, water, salt and pepper in a small skillet. Stir until the sugar dissolves. Cool the mixture and then pour over the cucumbers. Sprinkle with dill. Chill for several hours before serving. Yield: 6 to 8 servings

Summer

Cucumber Soup

   3 cups peeled, sliced cucumbers
   ½ onion, minced
   3 tablespoons butter
   2 cups chicken or vegetable broth
   1 tablespoon flour
   2 tablespoons lemon juice
   1 teaspoon dill
   1 cup plain yogurt
   1 small cucumber, seeded and grated

Sauté the cucumbers and onion in the butter. Add the other ingredients to the pan and simmer for ten minutes. Purée in food processor and chill. When ready to serve, stir in the yogurt and grated cucumber.
Yield: 4 servings

Raita (Indian Cucumber Salad)

   1 medium cucumber, peeled, cut in half, and seeded (or use burpless cucumber)
   ½ teaspoon salt
   ½ teaspoon cumin seed
   1 teaspoon fresh mint, minced
   salt and pepper to taste
   1 cup plain yogurt

Cover each cucumber half with ¼ teaspoon salt. Place face down on a paper towel for 30 minutes. Wipe the salt off the cucumber. Finely grate the cucumbers. Roast the cumin seeds in a small skillet over medium heat until they begin to brown. Cool to room temperature. Combine all the ingredients and chill for 1 hour.
Yield: 6 servings

Pickled Cucumbers

   2 ¼ pounds small, firm gherkin cucumbers
   2 cups preserving salt
   3 ¼ cups white-wine vinegar
   1 teaspoon dill seed
   2 sprigs tarragon
   4 ounces small pickling onions, peeled
   2 cloves garlic

Wash and dry the cucumbers, put them in a bowl and cover with the salt. Leave for 24 hours. Drain the cucumbers and rinse them in cold water. Drain and dry with a dish cloth, return to the bowl. Bring half the vinegar to boil, simmer for 5 minutes, then pour over the cucumbers. Cover and refrigerate for 24 hours. Drain the vinegar from the cucumbers into a saucepan and bring it to a boil, then set it aside to cool. Arrange the cucumbers in a glass jar, distributing the dill seed, tarragon, onions, and garlic as you fill the jar. Pour in the cool, drained vinegar, and top the jar with the remaining fresh vinegar. Cover with a lid and store in a cold place for 2 months before opening.

Cucumber Salad

  4 cucumbers, peeled and thinly sliced
  2 tablespoons rice-wine vinegar
  1 teaspoon coarse salt
  ½ teaspoon sugar
  1 small red onion, peeled and thinly sliced
  1 cup radishes, thinly sliced
  2 tablespoons chopped dill
  salt and pepper to taste

Put the cucumbers in a bowl and sprinkle with salt, vinegar, and sugar. Stir, cover, and let stand for 30 minutes. Drain off all the liquid, then rinse the cucumbers under cold water and pat them dry. Add the sliced onion, radishes, and dill. Toss. In a small bowl, whisk together the ingredients for the dressing. Add to the cucumbers. Season with salt and pepper. Serve slightly chilled.

White-Wine Dressing:

  ⅔ cup white-wine vinegar
  3 tablespoons sugar
  2 garlic cloves, minced or crushed
  1 tablespoon water
  3 tablespoons olive oil

Tomatoes

Growing Tip: Don't plant tomato seedlings until day and night temperatures are 50 degrees F. Stake or cage tomato plants. There are hundreds of varieties of tomatoes that fall into major categories of paste or sauce tomatoes, cherry tomatoes, slicing tomatoes, and yellow tomatoes. Green tomatoes are unripe tomatoes and not a separate type.

Cooking Tip: For making tomato sauce, use paste tomatoes. To peel and seed a tomato, cut an x in the bottom and plunge it into boiling water long enough to loosen the skin, about 20 to 30 seconds. Put the tomato in a bowl of ice water and peel. Halve the tomato lengthwise and squeeze out the seeds and juice. Last year, I planted currant tomatoes, a sweet, pearl-sized tomato that is delicious as a garnish or to snack on from a bowl. The green tomatoes you pick for cooking should be dark green and on the verge of just showing some pink.

Warm Cherry-Tomato Salad

    2 tablespoons balsamic vinegar
    2 tablespoons olive oil
    1 ¼ teaspoons minced garlic
    6 cups cherry tomatoes (can be different varieties)
    salt and pepper to taste
    ⅓ cup basil leaves, finely chopped

Heat the vinegar, oil, and garlic in a large skillet until just simmering. Add tomatoes and pepper and salt to taste. Cook for two minutes, tossing until slightly tender and heated through. Mix tomatoes with basil in a serving bowl.
Yield: 6 servings

Tomato, Parsley, and Red-Onion Salad

    1 pound tomatoes (about 3 medium-sized ones)
    ¼ teaspoon sugar
    ¼ teaspoon salt
    1 tablespoon olive oil
    1 teaspoon red-wine vinegar
    1 small red onion, sliced thin
    3 tablespoons chopped fresh parsley

Cut the tomatoes into ¼-inch-thick slices and arrange half the slices in one layer in a shallow serving dish. Combine the sugar and salt and sprinkle the layer of tomatoes with half the mixture. Arrange the remaining tomato slices on top and sprinkle with remaining sugar mixture. Combine the oil and vinegar and drizzle over the tomatoes. Let them stand at room temperature for 30 minutes. Sprinkle with the parsley and arrange the onion, separated into rings, on top.
Yield: 4 servings

Tomato Coulis

    tomatoes
    chives
    salt and pepper

Purée cored fresh tomatoes in a food processor. In a bowl, combine the purée with chives as desired and season with salt and pepper.

Tomato Sauce

¼ cup olive oil
3 cups chopped onions
2 cups grated carrots
1 tablespoon crushed garlic
12 cups peeled, seeded, and coarsely chopped tomatoes, with juice
salt to taste
1 teaspoon freshly ground black pepper
1 tablespoon minced basil
1 tablespoon oregano

Heat the oil in a deep pot and sauté the onions and carrots over medium heat until soft, 4 to 5 minutes. Stir in the garlic. Add the tomatoes and bring to a simmer. Stir in salt, pepper, basil, and oregano. Simmer to reduce and thicken, about 10 to 15 minutes. Do not overcook. Transfer to the bowl of a food processor and process mixture to a coarse texture.
Yield: 12 cups

Gazpacho

6 tomatoes, peeled and chopped
2 small cucumbers, peeled and chopped
1 teaspoon dill
3 tablespoons lemon juice
¾ cup of tomato juice
1 tablespoon olive oil
salt and pepper to taste

Purée all of the above ingredients in a food processor until chopped and blended.
Yield: 4 servings

Fried Green Tomatoes

2 green tomatoes
1 tablespoon sugar
½ cup flour
2 tablespoons butter

Slice the tomatoes ½ inch thick. Sprinkle lightly with sugar. Coat both sides of slices with flour. Fry in butter, drain.
Yield: 2 to 4 servings

Pasta with Fried Green Tomatoes and Chèvre

  3 or 4 large green tomatoes
  flour for dredging
  salt and pepper to taste
  olive oil
  1 pound spaghettini
  olive oil for tossing pasta
  1 cup soft chèvre

Slice green tomatoes no more than ¼ inch thick. Season flour with salt and pepper and dredge the tomato slices. Fry the slices in olive oil until nicely browned, adding oil as needed. You will probably have to fry the tomatoes in more than one batch. Cook the spaghettini. Drain and toss with a little olive oil to prevent sticking. Serve the pasta with the tomatoes and chèvre on top.
Yield: 4 servings

Tabbouleh

  2 cups bulghur or cracked wheat
  1 ½ cups orange juice
  1 ½ cups tomatoes, seeded and chopped
  1 cup minced fresh parsley
  ½ cup minced fresh mint
  ½ cup minced scallions
  ½ cup olive oil

salt and pepper to taste

Cover the bulghur with orange juice and let it stand until fluffy. Drain well. Add the other ingredients to bulghur and stir. Chill for several hours before serving.

Yield: 6 servings

Salsa

4 medium tomatoes, peeled and diced small
6 scallions, chopped
1 clove garlic, chopped fine
½ teaspoon basil
2 mild green chili peppers, seeded and chopped
½ teaspoon fresh oregano, finely chopped
1 jalapeño pepper, roasted, peeled, and finely chopped
½ teaspoon sugar
1 tablespoon chopped parsley
1 tablespoon lime juice
1 tablespoon fresh cilantro, finely chopped
1 tablespoon red-wine vinegar

Combine all the ingredients in a bowl. Season to taste with salt and pepper. Cover and chill several hours. Drain off excess liquid before serving.

Yield: 3 cups

Sun-dried Tomatoes

2 pounds plum tomatoes
1 garlic clove
salt to taste
olive oil

Preheat the oven to 200 degrees and line a baking sheet with aluminum foil. Cut the tomatoes in half lengthwise without slicing all the way through. Open the tomatoes and remove their seeds and then drain them upside down on paper towels. Set a baking rack on top of the foil-lined baking sheet and arrange the tomatoes, cut-side up, on the rack. Sprinkle each with a little salt. Bake the tomatoes, leaving the oven door open slightly. Bake until the tomatoes are shriveled and deep red, about 6 to 7 hours. Do not let tomatoes burn or get crisp. Cool the tomatoes and then pack in a sterilized jar, add garlic clove, and cover with olive oil.

Tomato Soup with Tarragon

    4 tablespoons butter
    1 small onion, chopped
    ½ clove garlic, finely chopped
    1 ½ pounds ripe tomatoes, peeled and chopped
    ⅔ cup dry white wine
    ½ cup tomato juice
    1 teaspoon sugar
    1 tablespoon tarragon leaves, chopped

Melt half the butter in a saucepan. Stir in the onion and garlic and cook gently for 3 minutes. Add the tomatoes, wine, sugar, salt, and half the tarragon. Cover and cook for 25 to 30 minutes. Cool slightly and purée in a food processor. Return to the saucepan and add the remaining tarragon, cook until heated through.

Yield: 4 servings

Tomato Ketchup

    6 pounds ripe tomatoes, cored and cut into wedges
    1 red onion, peeled and cut into wedges
    1 carrot, peeled and chopped
    1 teaspoon mustard seed
    1 ½ teaspoons ground cloves
    1 ½ teaspoons ground mace
    1 ½ teaspoons pepper
    1 ½ teaspoons celery salt
    ½ cup brown sugar
    1 tablespoon molasses
    1 clove garlic, sliced
    1 cup malt or apple-cider vinegar

Heat the oil in a heavy saucepan, add the tomatoes, onions, and carrot. Bring to a simmer. Cook slowly for 45 minutes. Mash tomatoes and stir frequently to prevent burning. Purée in blender. Return to saucepan and add spices, molasses, vinegar, and brown sugar. Stir until well blended and cook until mixture thickens and is reduced. (Cooking time depends on juiciness of the tomatoes.) Ladle ketchup into 2 or 3 pint canning jars and seal. Cool to room temperature. Ketchup can be stored in the refrigerator up to three months.

Uncooked Tomato Sauce

 4 pounds tomatoes, peeled, seeded, and diced
 2 scallions, white part only, minced
 2 cloves garlic, minced
 5 basil leaves, minced
 10 parsley springs, chopped fine
 2 tablespoons fresh oregano, minced
 ½ pound Taleggio or mozzarella cheese cut into 1-inch cubes
 1 tablespoon lemon juice
 3 tablespoons olive oil
 salt and pepper to taste

Combine the tomatoes, scallions, garlic, basil, parsley, lemon juice, oregano, and cheese in a bowl. Stir in olive oil and season with salt and pepper. Serve on lettuce, pasta, or garlic bread.
Yield: 3 cups

Chaiwalla's Famous Tomato Pie

Biscuit Pie Crust:

 2 cups flour
 4 teaspoons baking powder
 1 teaspoon salt
 ¼ cup butter
 ⅔ cup milk

Filling:

 ripe tomatoes, peeled (enough to cover dough)
 2 tablespoons torn basil leaves
 1 tablespoon chopped chives
 1 ½ cups grated cheddar cheese
 ⅓ cup mayonnaise

Preheat the oven to 400 degrees.
Place flour and baking powder in a bowl and cut in the butter until mixture becomes coarse. Add milk to make the mixture medium-soft. Place half the dough on a floured board and roll to fit a 9-inch pie pan. Cover dough with tomato slices. Sprinkle with basil and chives. Top with half the cheese and spread with mayonnaise. Add the remaining cheese. Roll the rest of the dough to fit over the top of the pie and pinch the crusts together. Bake until brown on top, about 20 minutes.
Yield: 6 servings

The Kitchen Gardener's Cookbook

Zucchini

Growing Tip: You only need to plant two hills of zucchini to reap a manageable harvest. Two or three plants will give up all the zucchini you need. Pick zucchini when they are small.

Cooking Tip: Zucchini can be exchanged for cucumber to use in salads. Squash blossoms are colorful and tasty additions to scrambled eggs. The blossoms can be dipped in batter and fried.

Stuffed Zucchini

    4 medium zucchini
    4 tablespoons melted butter
    ½ cup grated Parmesan cheese
    1 garlic clove, minced
    ¼ teaspoon oregano
    1½ cups soft bread crumbs

Trim the ends off and parboil the zucchini for 10 minutes in salted water. Cut in half lengthwise. Scoop out pulp (being careful to leave skins intact), place in bowl, and mix with remaining ingredients. Add salt and pepper to taste. Stuff the reserved skins and place in a greased baking dish for 15 to 20 minutes at 350 degrees. Place under broiler for a few minutes to brown.
Yield: 6 servings

Steamed Zucchini

    6 zucchini, thinly sliced
    6 tablespoons olive oil
    2 tablespoons red-wine vinegar
    ½ teaspoon mace
    salt and pepper to taste

Steam the zucchini until tender. Rinse under cold water. Drain and chill. Mix together the oil, vinegar, mace, and salt and pepper; pour over the zucchini.
Yield: 4 servings

🌿 Summer

Zucchini Bread

    3 cups grated zucchini
    1 cup vegetable oil
    1 ½ cups sugar
    3 eggs, beaten
    1 teaspoon vanilla
    3 cups flour
    1 teaspoon baking soda
    1 ½ teaspoons baking powder
    1 ½ teaspoons cinnamon
    ½ teaspoon salt
    1 cup chopped walnuts (optional)
    1 cup raisins (optional)

Mix together the grated zucchini, oil, sugar, eggs, and vanilla. Sift together the flour, baking powder, baking soda, cinnamon, and salt. Stir with other ingredients to blend. Add the nuts and raisins. Mix for 4 minutes. Pour into greased loaf pan and bake for 1 hour at 350 degrees.
Yield: 1 large loaf

Sautéed Zucchini

    4 zucchini, sliced into rounds
    3 tablespoons olive oil
    1 clove garlic, minced
    2 tablespoons minced scallions
    grated Parmesan cheese
    salt and pepper to taste

Heat the oil in a skillet and sauté the zucchini for 2 minutes, browning on both sides. Do not overcook. Turn off the heat and stir in the garlic and scallions. Transfer to serving dish. Sprinkle with Parmesan and salt and pepper to taste.
Yield: 4 servings

Marinated Baby Squash

    4 each 2-inch-long zucchini and yellow squash
    6 1-inch pattypans
    6 1-inch scallopini

The Kitchen Gardener's Cookbook

Marinade:
- ½ cup olive oil
- 2 tablespoons white-wine vinegar
- 2 teaspoons fresh thyme
- 4 bay leaves
- ½ teaspoon rosemary
- salt and pepper to taste

Steam the squash for 2 to 3 minutes. Mix the marinade ingredients together in a glass or ceramic bowl big enough to hold the squash. Add the squash to the marinade and turn them to coat well. Cover and leave at room temperature for 6 to 8 hours. Serve at room temperature.

Yield: 4 servings

Sesame Zucchini

- 4 medium-sized zucchini
- 2 tablespoon Asian sesame oil
- 3 teaspoons sesame seeds, toasted lightly
- 2 teaspoons soy sauce
- 2 tablespoons lemon juice

Halve the zucchini lengthwise and cut crosswise into ½-inch pieces. In a steamer set over simmering water, steam zucchini, covered, until tender, about 5 minutes. Toss the zucchini in a bowl with the oil and sesame seeds until coated well. Sprinkle with lemon juice. Serve warm or at room temperature.

Yield: 4 servings

Corn

Growing Tip: Start corn from seed. Plant seeds in groups of four as corn is wind-pollinated and pollen needs to reach each ear. Thin when they are 4 to 6 inches tall to a foot between each plant.

Cooking Tip: Harvest corn as soon as it is ripe. Steam until it is just tender.

Grilled Corn

- 16 ears shucked baby corn or 8 ears shucked young corn
- ¼ cup olive oil

       salt and pepper to taste

Brush the corn with olive oil. Light a charcoal fire in an open grill. Run skewers crosswise through the centers of the corn. When the charcoal is ready, grill the corn, turning frequently. When kernels are tender, sprinkle with salt and pepper to taste.

Corn-on-the-Cob

       2 ears of shucked corn per person
       butter
       salt and pepper to taste

Cook shucked corn in boiling UNSALTED water for 3 to 4 minutes. Serve with butter and salt and pepper.

Creamed Corn

Remove the kernels from uncooked corn. Cook the corn kernels over low heat in about ¼ cup of water or milk for about 5 minutes. Add butter and salt and pepper to taste.

Corn Salad

    3 cups cooked corn kernels
    ½ red pepper, diced
    ½ cup diced celery
    2 tablespoons chopped parsley
    ¼ cup vegetable oil
    ¼ cup wine vinegar
    2 tablespoons water
    salt and pepper

Combine the corn, pepper, celery, and parsley. Mix the vegetable oil, vinegar, and water, and salt and pepper to taste; pour over salad. Chill before serving.

Yield: 6 servings

Corn Fritters

    2 cups uncooked corn kernels
    3 eggs
    2 tablespoons milk or cream
    1 tablespoon melted butter
    1 ½ cups flour
    1 teaspoon baking powder
    1 tablespoon chopped chives (optional)
    salt and pepper to taste
    oil for frying

Beat the eggs and mix with corn, milk, melted butter, baking powder, chives, and salt and pepper; add enough flour to bind the fritters. Don't make the mixture too thin or too thick. Heat the oil in a skillet. Drop the batter by tablespoons in the hot oil and cook for 3 to 5 minutes. Drain on paper towels and serve.

Yield: 6 servings

Corn Pudding

    2 cups corn kernels
    2 tablespoons butter
    3 tablespoons flour
    ½ teaspoon sugar
    2 egg yolks

2 whole eggs
¼ cup milk
2 egg whites, beaten stiff
salt and pepper to taste

Melt butter in skillet and sauté the corn; add the sugar and salt and pepper. Remove from heat. Combine the egg yolks and 2 whole eggs and beat. Add to corn, stirring constantly. Mix in the flour. Fold the egg whites into the corn. Pour the mixture into a buttered casserole dish or pudding basin and bake at 375 degrees for 45 minutes until golden brown on top.
Yield: 4 servings

Corn Bread

½ cup flour
1 ½ cups milk or buttermilk
1 ½ cups corn meal
1 ½ cups cooked corn kernels
3 tablespoons butter, melted
2 eggs, beaten
2 teaspoons baking powder
2 tablespoons sugar
1 teaspoon baking soda

Preheat the oven to 375 degrees. Grease a loaf pan. Mix together the flour, baking powder, baking soda, and sugar. Mix in the cornmeal. In a different bowl, combine the milk or buttermilk, beaten eggs, melted butter, and corn. Combine the wet and dry ingredients and mix until just blended. Pour into the loaf pan. Bake for 25 minutes or until cake tester inserted in center comes out clean.
Yield: 1 loaf

Corn Chowder

1 onion, chopped
2 celery stalks, chopped
2 tablespoons vegetable oil
2 cups chicken or vegetable broth
2 ½ cups water
1 ½ cups boiling potatoes, peeled and cut into ½-inch cubes
4 cups corn kernels (about 6 ears of corn)

The Kitchen Gardener's Cookbook

  2 teaspoons thyme leaves, minced
  salt and pepper to taste

In a kettle or large saucepan, cook the onion and celery in the oil, stir until soft. Add the broth, water, and potatoes and simmer for 10 minutes. Add corn and the thyme leaves. Add salt and pepper to taste. Simmer until potatoes are tender. Purée 2 cups of the chowder in a food processor and stir into the remaining chowder.

Yield: 4 to 6 servings

Corn Relish

  4 cups cooked corn kernels
  1 red pepper, minced
  1 green pepper, minced
  4 stalks celery, sliced
  1 sweet onion, chopped
  ¼ cup sugar
  1 tablespoon mustard seed
  1 tablespoon salt
  ½ cup white-wine vinegar
  ½ cup water

Parboil the peppers and celery for 5 minutes, then drain. Add the onion and corn to the celery and peppers. In a different saucepan, combine the sugar, salt, mustard seed, vinegar, and water. Bring to a boil then reduce to a simmer. Add the vegetables and simmer for 15 minutes. Pour into sterilized jars and seal. Or chill the relish and serve immediately.

Yield: 4 pints

Peppers

Growing Tip: Leave a little of the stem attached when you pick peppers. The two varieties are sweet and hot. Hot peppers are also known as chili peppers. Peppers like heat and water.

Cooking Tip: Place chili peppers flat on a cookie sheet and freeze, then transfer the peppers to plastic bags and return to freezer. Make sure to remove seeds and veins of peppers. Seeds and veins are the hottest parts of chili peppers.

Sautéed Peppers

    2 large green bell peppers
    2 large red bell peppers
    ¼ cup olive oil
    2 cloves garlic, minced
    1 tablespoon chopped parsley
    salt and pepper to taste

Sauté the peppers and garlic in the oil about 5 minutes. Add the parsley.
Yield: 4 servings

Stuffed Peppers

    2 green bell peppers
    1 small onion
    ½ pound lean ground beef chuck (optional)
    ½ cup bread crumbs
    2 tablespoons parsley, minced
    1 garlic clove, minced
    ¼ cup water
    ¼ cup cooked rice
    salt and pepper to taste
    1 ½ cups tomato sauce

Mix together the ground beef, onion, bread crumbs, salt and pepper, parsley, garlic, rice, and water. Cut the pepper in half lengthwise, remove core and seed, fill with the mixture, and place in buttered casserole. Pour the tomato sauce over the peppers and bake, covered, at 350 degrees for an hour; uncover and cook for another 15 minutes.
Yield: 4 servings

Red Pepper Soubise

    ¼ cup olive oil
    2 onions, cut into chunks
    2 tablespoons sage, chopped fine
    4 red bell peppers, roasted, seeded, and chopped

Heat the oil in a skillet and sauté the onions slowly until soft, stirring often. Purée the onions, sage, and peppers in a food processor until smooth. Add salt and pepper to taste. Serve as a sauce or spread on pizza or use as an appetizer with crackers.

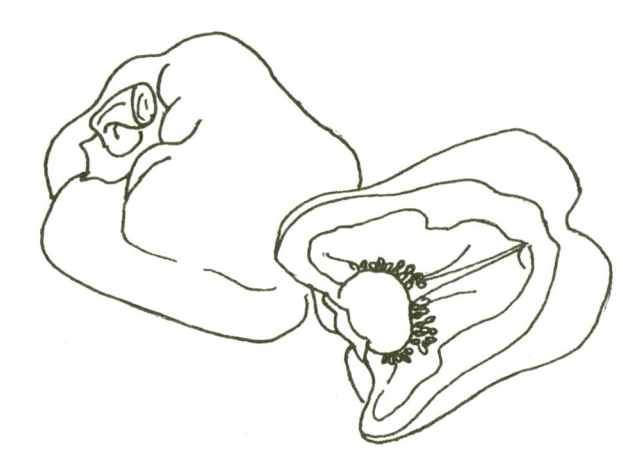

Baked Yellow Peppers and Tomatoes

    3 yellow bell peppers
    3 ripe tomatoes
    ¼ cup olive oil
    3 cloves garlic, minced
    2 teaspoons thyme, minced
    salt and pepper to taste

Cut the peppers in half lengthwise. Remove the cores and seed. Cut the peppers into strips 1 ½ inches wide. Core the tomatoes and cut them into slices ½ inch thick. Arrange the peppers and tomatoes in a baking dish. Blend the olive oil, garlic, thyme, and salt and pepper. Pour over the tomatoes and peppers. Bake in a moderate oven for 1 hour and 15 minutes until the peppers are tender. Allow to cool to room temperature before serving.
Yield: 6 servings

Roasted Peppers

To roast peppers: Preheat the broiler. Cover the broiler pan with a sheet of aluminum foil and spread the peppers on it. Place them as close to flame as possible. Turn the peppers frequently so that they are charred and blistered all over, about 5 minutes on each side. Place the peppers in a brown paper bag and let cool. Peel the charred skin from the peppers; seed and core the peppers.

Peppers and Basil

    1 pound red and yellow bell peppers
    2 to 3 tablespoons olive oil
    2 tablespoons pine nuts
    1 to 2 tablespoons lemon juice
    2 teaspoons chopped basil

Roast the peppers. When cool, peel and cut the peppers into strips; discard the seeds and stem. Arrange strips on a serving plate. Heat the oil in a small skillet, and add the pine nuts. Cook, stirring, until the nuts are brown. Add the lemon juice. Spoon the mixture over the peppers, add salt and pepper to taste. Garnish with basil.
Yield: 4 servings

Red Pepper and Eggplant Dip

    1 medium eggplant
    2 pounds red bell peppers
    8 tablespoons olive oil
    4 garlic cloves, minced
    3 tablespoons lemon juice
    1 small jalapeño chili pepper, seeded and minced

Preheat oven to 400 degrees. Coat eggplant and peppers with half the oil and arrange in a jellyroll pan. Roast the vegetables, turning a few times for 30 to 40 minutes until eggplant is soft and peppers are charred. Transfer the peppers to a bowl and cover with plastic wrap until cool. Peel and seed the peppers. Peel the eggplant and put pulp into bowl of food processor. Add peppers, remaining 4 tablespoons of olive oil, lemon juice, garlic, jalapeño, and salt and pepper to taste. Combine well. Transfer the mixture to a saucepan and simmer, stirring frequently, 15 to 20 minutes, until thickened. Cool dip and chill, covered, for 24 hours before serving. Serve with pita triangles.
Yield: 2 cups

The Kitchen Gardener's Cookbook

Spinach

Growing Tip: Plant a small row of spinach in the spring for an early crop. Plant another in late August and let it winter over. If you cover it with a cold frame, you can have spinach in March. Spinach likes cool, sandy soil. Harvest spinach close to the crown and it will grow again. You can harvest spinach leaves individually or pick the whole plant.

Growing Tip: Spinach, chard, and sorrel can be interchanged in most recipes. Wash spinach well to remove all sand and dirt. Use spinach stems whenever you can in recipes.

Spinach and Garlic Salad

    1 tablespoon olive oil
    3 large garlic cloves sliced thin lengthwise
    3 large bunches of spinach
    salt and pepper to taste

Wash spinach and discard coarse stems. Heat the oil in a heavy 8-quart kettle until hot but not smoking and add the garlic and the spinach. Sauté the garlic and the spinach, turn with tongs until spinach is wilted but still green, about 2 minutes. Add salt and pepper to taste.

Warm Spinach Salad with Arugula

    1 large bunch spinach, coarse stems discarded, leaves washed well, spun dry, and torn into bite-sized pieces
    2 cups arugula leaves, washed well and spun dry
    4 tablespoons olive oil
    4 scallions, sliced thin
    4 tablespoons red-wine vinegar
    2 teaspoons sugar
    salt and pepper to taste

Arrange spinach and arugula leaves in a salad bowl. Heat olive oil in a skillet, add the scallions, and sauté until soft. Add the vinegar, sugar, and salt and pepper to taste, stirring until heated through. Pour the mixture over the spinach and arugula.
Yield: 4 to 6 servings

Summer

Spinach and Bacon Salad

    ¾ pound spinach, coarse stems discarded, leaves washed and spun dry
    3 slices bacon, cooked until crisp, drained and crumbled
    2 scallions, minced
    ½ cup crumbled blue cheese
    2 hard-cooked eggs, chopped

In a salad bowl, toss together all ingredients. Drizzle with following salad dressing and mix well.
Yield: 4 servings

Lemon Dressing:

    ¼ cup fresh lemon juice
    1 tablespoon mayonnaise
    ½ teaspoon dry mustard
    ¼ teaspoon sugar
    salt and pepper to taste
    1 small garlic clove, chopped
    1 cup olive oil

Blend all the ingredients in a food processor except the olive oil. When the ingredients are smooth, add the olive oil in a stream until well blended. Transfer dressing to a jar and keep covered, chilled, until ready to serve.
Yield: 1 ¼ cups

Creamed Spinach

    1 ½ cups spinach, chopped
    2 tablespoons grated horseradish
    2 tablespoons butter
    ¼ cup plain yogurt or sour cream
    ½ teaspoon nutmeg
    salt and pepper to taste

Cook the spinach until wilted in saucepan with boiling water. (Spinach can also be steamed.) Drain well. Combine in a bowl with other ingredients, transfer to casserole or other oven-proof dish, and heat.
Yield: 4 servings

Cream of Spinach Soup

    1 cup cooked spinach
    1 tablespoon chopped onion
    ¼ cup parsley
    3 tablespoons butter
    2 tablespoons flour
    salt and pepper to taste
    2 cups of light cream
    2 cups chicken or vegetable broth

Melt the butter in a large saucepan and stir in the flour and salt and pepper to taste. Cook for 3 minutes. Place all the other ingredients in a blender and purée. Add to the flour mixture and heat. Do not boil.
Yield: 4 servings

Potatoes

Growing Tip: Most market potatoes have been treated not to sprout. Buy seed potatoes for planting. Cut the potatoes in 4 or 5 pieces with at least 2 eyes in each piece. Dry them for several days, until no moisture is evident; plant with eyes facing up in 4 to 5 inches of soil.

Cooking Tip: Leave the skin on potatoes whenever possible. Scrub well. There are several varieties of potatoes: blue, red, russet or Idaho, white. Try to use the type of potato specified in recipes. Red potatoes are good for boiling. Idaho (russet) is a baking potato.

Parslied New Potatoes

    2 tablespoons butter
    2 pounds new potatoes, washed and halved
    ¼ cup fresh parsley or chives, chopped
    ⅔ cup dry white wine
    ¼ teaspoon paprika
    salt and pepper to taste

Place butter in a baking dish, melt in 400-degree oven. Add potatoes, herbs, and wine. Toss to coat. Cover and return to oven for 40 minutes or until potatoes are tender, basting every 15 minutes.
Yield: 4 servings

Dilled Potatoes

 1 pound small red boiling potatoes, scrubbed
 ¼ teaspoon dry mustard
 1 tablespoon white-wine vinegar
 1 ½ teaspoons dry white wine
 salt to taste
 2 tablespoons olive oil
 ¼ cup minced dill
 pepper to taste

Cut the potatoes lengthwise in quarters. In a steamer set over boiling water, steam them, covered for 7 to 10 minutes or until they are tender. In a bowl, whisk together the mustard, vinegar, wine, and salt to taste. Add the oil in a stream and whisk the dressing until well combined. Add the potatoes while they are still warm and toss them gently with the dressing, the dill, and pepper to taste until they are well coated. Let the mixture stand, tossing occasionally, for 30 minutes, then serve it at room temperature.
Yield: 4 servings

German Potato Salad

 2 pounds light (boiling) potatoes, quartered lengthwise and cut into ¾-inch pieces
 1 onion chopped fine
 2 tablespoons olive oil
 ½ cup distilled white-wine vinegar
 ½ cup broth, beef, chicken, or vegetable
 ⅓ cup parsley, minced

In a steamer set over boiling water, steam the potatoes, covered, for 10 to 12 minutes or until they are tender; and transfer them to a bowl. While the potatoes are steaming, sauté the onion in the oil in a skillet, stirring occasionally, until golden in color. Remove the skillet from the heat and add the vinegar and broth. Bring the mixture to a boil and cook until reduced to about ⅔ of a cup. Add to the potatoes with the parsley and combine.
Yield: 6 servings

Picnic Potato Salad

    1 pound light potatoes, (yellow-fleshed), quartered lengthwise and cut into ¾-inch pieces
    1 tablespoon white-wine vinegar
    2 tablespoons Dijon-style mustard
    salt and pepper to taste
    1 small onion, chopped
    3 stalks celery, leaves and strings removed, chopped
    ¼ cup red bell pepper, chopped

Cook the potatoes in a steamer, covered for 10 to 12 minutes, or until they are tender. Transfer them to a bowl and let cool. In another bowl, whisk together the vinegar, mustard, and salt and pepper to taste; add the oil in a stream, whisking until the dressing is emulsified. Add the dressing to the potatoes with the onion, the bell pepper, and the celery and combine the salad well.
Yield: 6 servings

Roasted Potatoes

    3 tablespoons olive oil
    1 pound small new potatoes
    6 cloves garlic
    salt and pepper to taste

Scrub the potatoes and pat dry. Place in an oven-proof casserole with a tight-fitting lid. Add the other ingredients and mix well so the potatoes are coated with oil. Cover and bake for 50 minutes.
Yield: 4 servings

Potato and Sugar-Snap Peas

    1 ½ pounds small red potatoes, quartered
    3 tablespoons lemon juice
    salt and pepper to taste
    ½ pound sugar-snap peas, strings removed and the pods cut in half
    ⅓ cup olive oil
    ½ teaspoon dry mustard
    1 tablespoon minced parsley

Steam the potatoes, covered, for 8 to 12 minutes, or until tender. Transfer to a serving bowl and toss with 1 tablespoon of the lemon juice

Summer

and salt and pepper to taste. Blanch the snap peas in a saucepan of boiling water for 5 seconds. Drain under running cold water. Whisk together the remaining 2 tablespoons lemon juice and the mustard. Add the oil in a slow stream, whisking until combined. Add the snap peas to the potatoes. Sprinkle with parsley and stir in the dressing, tossing well. Serve at room temperature.
Yield: 4 servings

New Potatoes and Mint

- 12 very small new red potatoes
- zest of 1 lemon
- ¼ cup olive oil
- 2 tablespoons lemon juice
- 3 cloves garlic, minced
- ¼ cup chopped mint
- salt and pepper to taste

Cook the potatoes in 4 quarts salted boiling water until tender, 20 to 30 minutes. Drain. Heat the oil in a large skillet. Add the potatoes and sauté until golden brown. Add the lemon juice and toss well. Combine the grated lemon, garlic, and mint, toss with the potatoes. Season with salt and pepper.
Yield: 6 servings

New Potatoes in Chive Butter

- 3 tablespoons unsalted butter, softened
- ½ cup chopped chives
- salt and pepper to taste
- 3 pounds small new potatoes

In a large bowl, combine the butter, chives, and salt and pepper to taste. In a large saucepan with salted water to cover by 1 inch, add potatoes and simmer until tender, 15 to 20 minutes. Drain the potatoes in a colander and add to the butter mixture. Toss to combine.
Yield: 6 servings

Potato Salad with Arugula

- 6 medium-sized red potatoes, cubed
- 2 tablespoons vinegar
- 1 tablespoon olive oil

2 hard-cooked eggs, chopped
1 green onion, chopped
1 cup sugar-snap peas, cut up
12 arugula leaves

Boil the potatoes until tender, about 10 minutes. Drain. Add vinegar, olive oil, chopped eggs, onion, sugar-snap peas, and arugula. Toss well. Serve at room temperature.

Yield: 4 servings

Cabbage

Growing Tip: Cabbage is easy to grow and great in salads. It can be replanted for a late-fall or early-spring crop. Plant marigolds near cabbage to discourage cabbage moths.

Cooking Tip: Don't overcook cabbage as it can become soggy and flavorless. Soak cabbage in salted cold water to make it crisp. Cut out the stem and core before using cabbage.

Coleslaw

1 large head cabbage
1 small onion, grated
2 carrots, coarsely grated
1 ½ tablespoons red-wine vinegar
¼ cup mayonnaise
2 tablespoons plain yogurt
½ tablespoon sugar
1 teaspoon celery seeds
1 teaspoon dry mustard
salt and pepper to taste

Wash and core the cabbage and shred into a bowl. Add the carrots and the grated onion to the bowl. In a saucepan, boil the vinegar, mayonnaise, yogurt, sugar, celery seeds, mustard, and salt and pepper to taste. Toss the dressing with the cabbage until well mixed. Chill before serving.

Yield: 6 servings

Cabbage Salad

    4 slices bacon
    3 scallions, finely chopped
    1 small head green cabbage
    3 tablespoons red-wine vinegar
    1 teaspoon sugar
    salt and pepper to taste
    2 tablespoons chopped parsley

Wash the cabbage, remove outer leaves and inner core. Shred the cabbage. Cook the bacon in a large skillet until crisp. Drain on a paper towel, then crumble into large pieces. Remove all but 2 tablespoons of the bacon fat from the skillet and cook the scallions in it until transparent. Add the shredded cabbage and cook, stirring until the cabbage begins to wilt. Add the bacon and wine vinegar. Stir in the sugar. Add salt and pepper to taste. Serve, garnished with parsley.
Yield: 4 servings

Braised Red Cabbage

    ¼ pound bacon, cut into small pieces
    1 large onion, diced
    2 medium apples, cored and diced
    1 large head red cabbage, cored, quartered, and sliced
    1 cup chicken or vegetable broth
    ¼ cup cider vinegar
    ½ cup brown sugar
    1 medium potato, peeled

Preheat the oven to 350 degrees. Cook the bacon in a deep oven-proof skillet with an oven-proof cover until softened. Add the onion and cook until translucent. Add apples, cabbage, broth, vinegar, and brown sugar. Stir while bringing to a boil. Cover and put into oven and cook until the cabbage is tender, about 1 hour. Remove from oven and finely grate the potato into the pan. Stir until the potato has thickened the braising liquid into a sauce, cooking over medium heat for a couple of minutes if necessary. Add salt and pepper to taste.
Yield: 6 to 8 servings

Bubble and Squeak

    4 cups cooked mashed potatoes
    4 cups cooked cabbage
    4 tablespoons olive or vegetable oil
    salt and pepper to taste

Mix the potatoes and cabbage, and season with salt and pepper to taste. Sauté over medium heat. Press and flatten the vegetables with the back of a spoon so that they form a flat cake. Brown one side, then turn and brown the other. Transfer to a plate and serve immediately.
Yield: 6 servings

Fall

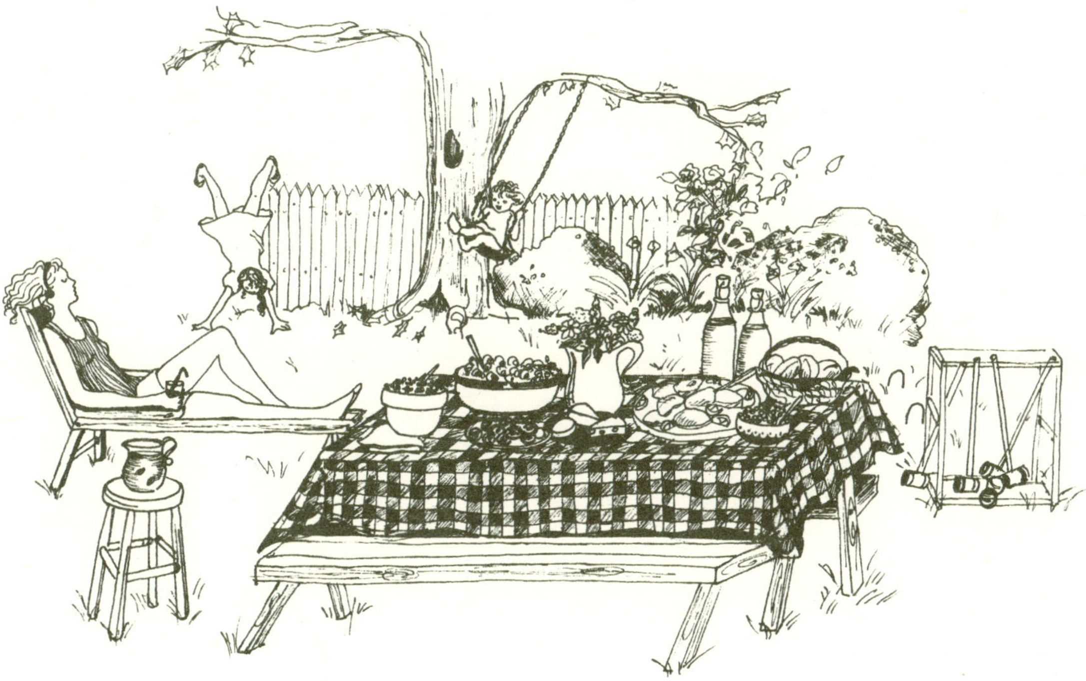

The Kitchen Gardener's Cookbook

Fall

Gardens and children mark time's passage. On our property, vague and imagined outlines of flower and vegetable beds, plantings of shrubs and fruit trees have become distinct and established realities after eighteen years of planning and care. The divided irises and peonies have spread along the fence. Spindly lilacs, dug up and planted in a different part of the yard from their parents, have grown into tall bushes. The little girls spinning cartwheels across the lawn who turned into teenagers sprawled on lawn chairs, faces lifted to the sun, music throbbing through head phones, are now young women who say to me, "I want to learn about gardening."

When fall comes and the garden offers its final bright bouquets and produce, I think back to the beginning of the season when snow drops dipped creamy ovals over the last patches of muddy snow, and parsley and chives recalled the color green, and the cat sat for hours on the terrace waiting for the chipmunk she remembered from last summer to emerge from its hole.

Spring has as much to do with nostalgia as it does with rebirth, just as autumn brings hope along with the arrival of dormancy. "Next year," I say to myself as I mound dirt around the roses and cut back the perennials and pull up the withered tomato stalks, "I'll start the peas earlier. I'll plant ever-bearing raspberries. I'll try a different kind of eggplant." My husband and I carry the picnic table and benches to the garage. I remember the midsummer celebration we had when the girls were home for a visit. My parents and two older sisters came, my little sister and her husband and three small boys were here from North Carolina, my best friend and her husband and two sons joined the party, so did our next-door neighbors and their little girl.

Big bowls of pasta salad, green salads, cold chicken poached with herbs and lemon, sliced tomatoes, and plates of cheeses, fresh bread, and bowls of blueberries and raspberries covered the picnic table. From the lawn, the clok, clok of croquet mallets against balls, an excited voice calling, "You're poison!", laughter and chatter from the adults gathered on the terrace filled the warm, dusky air.

Now the air is edged with cold. My husband gets the ladder and leans it against the Norway maple's ample trunk to take down the swing that hangs from a long, low branch. We put up the swing the first year we lived in the house. My daughters swung there through the seasons until their legs grew too long and the motion of leaving the earth and rising into the air no longer claimed their interest. The chains have rusted, the push and drag of swingers' feet have polished a circle of bare ground under the tree. My daughters have left home and flown to distant places to try their wings. We still hang the swing each year — these days for the little girl next door, for visiting nephews, and as a reminder of our own daughters. I think of them taking turns, one pressing her toes against the dirt for the take-off, calling to her sister, "Push harder," as she tried to reach the canopy of green above her. That canopy is a brilliant show of color in October. I've picked the last bunches of herbs to dry and wished the squash into ripeness before the cold weather settles in for good. Needles from the white pine beside the kitchen garden drift slowly, carried on sunlit currents of wind. Soon the garden is buried under a soft, brown blanket. I put away my gardening gloves and hang up my trowel. My work of putting the garden to bed is done.

Root Vegetables

Growing Tip: Root vegetables remain to be harvested long after the frost has withered everything else in the garden.

Cooking Tip: The most brightly colored root vegetables are often the healthiest, such as carrots, beets, and yams.

Roasted Root Vegetables

4 potatoes, cubed
2 turnips, cubed
1 acorn squash, peeled and cubed
2 carrots, cleaned and sliced into small pieces
1 parsnip, cleaned and sliced
1 onion, chopped into large pieces
1 red pepper, cored, seeded, and sliced into $\frac{1}{3}$-inch-wide strips
¼ cup olive oil
3 tablespoons salt

Place vegetables in an oven-proof baking dish and toss with olive oil and salt. Bake in a 350-degree oven for an hour or until the vegetables

are tender and slightly browned. Toss occasionally while cooking to prevent sticking.
Yield: 4 servings

Gratin of Winter Root Vegetables

    2 parsnips
    2 turnips
    2 rutabagas
    2 sweet potatoes
    2 bunches sorrel or 1 bunch spinach
    1 ½ cups heavy cream
    salt and pepper to taste

Preheat the oven to 375 degrees. Peel the root vegetables and cut them into ½-inch-thick slices. Remove the stems from the sorrel or spinach. Fill a baking dish or oven-proof casserole with the cut-up vegetables. Pour in the cream and sprinkle on salt and pepper to taste. Cover the vegetables with the sorrel or spinach. Cover the casserole and bake for 45 minutes until the vegetables are tender.
Yield: 6 servings

Winter-Vegetable Purée

    3 cups celery root, trimmed, peeled, and cut into ½-inch cubes
    2 medium-sized baking potatoes, peeled and cut into 1-inch cubes
    2 medium-sized turnips, peeled and cut into ½-inch cubes
    4 medium-sized leeks, white part only, washed well and cut crosswise into 1-inch pieces
    salt and pepper to taste

Put the celery root, potatoes, turnips, and leeks in a saucepan of cold water and bring to a boil. Simmer until all the vegetables are tender, about 30 minutes. Drain well. Purée the vegetables in a food processor until smooth. Add salt and pepper to taste.
Yield: 4 servings

Parsnip, Potato, and Garlic Purée

    2 large parsnips, peeled and cut into ½-inch rounds
    2 large baking potatoes, peeled and cut into ½-inch cubes
    10 cloves garlic, roasted and peeled

½ cup low-fat milk
salt and pepper to taste

Place the parsnips in a saucepan and cover with water. Bring to a boil, then simmer for 5 minutes. Add the potatoes and cook until parsnips and potatoes are soft, about 15 minutes. Drain well and place in a food processor with the roasted garlic and the milk; process the mixture until well combined.

Yield: 4 servings

Vegetable Broth

2 heads celery root, rinsed, and coarsely chopped
2 large leeks, washed well and coarsely chopped
4 carrots, coarsely chopped
2 medium onions, coarsely chopped
2 gallons cold water
salt and pepper to taste

Combine the celery, leeks, onions, carrots and water in a stockpot. Bring the water to a boil and lower heat and simmer until the broth is reduced to 1 gallon, about 1 ½ hours. Strain through a fine sieve. Pour broth into a saucepan, bring to a boil, and reduce to 4 cups, about 45 minutes. Season with salt and pepper.

Yield: 4 cups

Winter Squash and Pumpkins

Growing Tip: Try planting different varieties of winter squash: Hubbard, Blue, Acorn, Munchkin, Turban, Sweetmeat, Delicata, and Banana to name a few.

Cooking Tip: Add cut-up winter squash to stews and soups for extra flavor and nutrition.

Butternut Squash and Cheese Purée

1 medium-sized butternut squash, peeled, and cut into ½-inch cubes
¼ cup Parmesan cheese

⚜ Fall

  2 tablespoons chicken or vegetable broth
  salt and pepper to taste

Place the squash in a saucepan and cover with cold water. Bring to a boil, then simmer until tender, about 15 minutes. Drain well. Place the squash in a food processor with the broth and the Parmesan cheese and salt and pepper to taste. Process until smooth.
Yield: 4 servings

Butternut Bisque

  1 small butternut squash, washed, cut in half, and seeded
  2 green apples, peeled, cored, and chopped
  1 medium onion, chopped
  ¼ teaspoon marjoram
  1 quart chicken or vegetable stock
  2 slices white bread, trimmed
  1 ½ teaspoons salt
  ¼ teaspoon pepper

Combine squash, apples, onion, marjoram, stock, bread, salt, and pepper in a heavy saucepan. Bring to a boil and simmer, uncovered, for 30 to 45 minutes. Scoop out flesh and seeds of squash, discard skins, and return the pulp to the soup. Purée the soup in a food processor until smooth. Return to saucepan and heat.
Yield: 4 to 6 servings

Orange-Butternut Squash Purée

  1 medium-size butternut squash, peeled and cut into ½-inch cubes
  1 teaspoon grated orange rind
  2 tablespoons orange juice
  salt and pepper to taste

Place the squash in a saucepan and cover with cold water. Bring to a boil, then simmer, until tender, about 15 minutes. Drain well. Place the squash in a food processor with orange juice and zest and salt and pepper to taste. Process until smooth.
Yield: 4 servings

Orange-Pumpkin Bread

½ medium or 1 small pumpkin
3 ½ cups flour
2 teaspoons baking soda
½ teaspoon salt
1 teaspoon cinnamon
1 teaspoon nutmeg
3 cups sugar
1 cup oil
2 eggs
⅔ cup orange juice
½ cup raisins (optional)

Quarter the pumpkin and steam it until soft. Discard seeds and stringy part. Scoop out the pulp and mash. Mix together the flour, baking soda, salt, cinnamon, and nutmeg. Add the oil, egg, orange juice, and mashed pumpkin and stir until just mixed. Stir in the raisins. Pour batter into 2 greased loaf pans. Bake at 350 degrees for 1 hour.
Yield: 2 loaves

Pumpkin Pie

½ medium pumpkin, quartered
3 eggs
⅔ cup brown sugar
1 ½ cups light cream
½ teaspoon ginger
½ teaspoon nutmeg
1 teaspoon cinnamon
½ teaspoon salt
1 teaspoon vanilla
1 uncooked pie shell

Steam pumpkin until soft. Discard seeds and stringy part. Scoop out flesh, put in food processor and purée. Mix purée with eggs, sugar, and cream until blended. Add ginger, cinnamon, nutmeg, salt, and vanilla. Pour the filling into pie shell and bake at 350 degrees for 35 minutes.

Pumpkin au Gratin

    1 2-pound pumpkin
    ¼ cup olive oil
    ½ cup flour
    2 garlic cloves, minced
    2 tablespoons parsley, minced
    ¼ teaspoon mace
    salt and pepper to taste

Preheat the oven to 350 degrees. Cut the pumpkin in half, peel, remove the seeds, and cut into ½-inch cubes. Evenly coat the cubes in flour. Oil the bottom and sides of a baking dish or oven-proof casserole with the olive oil. Fill the casserole with the pumpkin. Sprinkle with the garlic, parsley, mace, and salt and pepper to taste. Bake for 2 to 2½ hours.
Yield: 6 servings

Roasted Pumpkin Seeds

    1 cup seeds from a freshly cut pumpkin or winter squash
    2 tablespoons vegetable oil
    salt to taste

Preheat the oven to 325 degrees. Wash and dry the seeds, then heat the oil in a skillet and lightly brown the seeds. Remove with a slotted spoon and put a single layer on a cookie sheet. Salt to taste and then bake for 15 minutes or until crisp.
Yield: 1 cup

Brussels Sprouts

Growing Tip: Plant in early summer so that Brussels sprouts have time to develop. Brussels sprouts take about 4 months to grow from seed to harvest. They love cold weather and will continue to grow through first frosts. Smaller sprouts are milder than large ones.

Cooking Tip: Add a pinch of sugar to cooking water for Brussels sprouts.

Braised Brussels Sprouts

    4 slices bacon
    1 onion, chopped small
    3 cups small Brussels sprouts
    salt and pepper to taste

Cook the bacon in a skillet until crisp. Drain on a paper towel. Sauté the onion in the bacon fat until translucent. Add the Brussels sprouts and the salt and pepper to taste. Cover and cook for 5 minutes.
Yield: 4 servings

Brussels Sprouts and Spinach Salad

    4 slices bacon
    1 pint Brussels sprouts
    1 ½ teaspoons caraway seeds
    3 tablespoons vegetable oil
    3 tablespoons white-wine vinegar
    ¼ teaspoon sugar
    ½ pound spinach, stems discarded, washed, and dried

Cook the bacon in a skillet until it is crisp, drain on paper towels. Heat the fat and sauté the Brussels sprouts with the caraway seeds, stirring, for 1 to 2 minutes, until the sprouts are tender. Remove the skillet from the heat and add the oil, vinegar, sugar, and spinach. Sauté for 1 minute or until the spinach has wilted.
Yield: 4 servings

Brussels Sprouts with Bacon, Onion, and Carrots

    1 pint Brussels sprouts
    2 slices of bacon
    1 medium onion, chopped
    1 carrot, peeled and cut into matchsticks
    salt and pepper to taste

Wash and trim Brussels sprouts. Cut each sprout from stem to top end into sixths, or if they are small, into fourths. Cook bacon in frying pan, stirring occasionally. If there is a lot of fat, pour some off but leave enough for sautéing the remaining ingredients. Add onions and cook until translucent. Add sprouts and carrots and sauté, stirring occasionally, until tender but crisp. Add salt and pepper to taste.
Yield: 4 servings

Fall

Steamed Brussels Sprouts with Apples

    1 pint Brussels sprouts
    1 tablespoon butter (more if needed)
    1 shallot, chopped
    1 apple, peeled, cored, and chopped

Wash and trim Brussels sprouts. Score the bottom of each one with an x. Sauté shallot in butter until translucent. Add apple and cook through. Keep warm. Steam the sprouts over boiling water until just done. Toss with apple mixture. Add salt and pepper to taste.
Yield: 4 servings

Dried Beans and Shelling Beans

Growing Tip: Leave dry beans on the vine until they are dry or pull the whole bean plant and hang to dry.

Cooking Tip: These are great to use in soups and casseroles. Cranberry beans are great to use in Italian soups. Jacob's cattle beans make great baked beans.

Black-Bean Turkey Soup

    1 cup dried black beans
    2 quarts turkey soup (chicken or vegetable soup may be substituted)

Rinse the beans and cover with cold water and let soak at least 6 hours. (Black beans need less soaking time than other beans.) Drain and rinse well. Cover with cold water and bring to a simmer, stirring occasionally until done. Add water in small amounts if too much evaporates. Heat the soup. When the beans are done, add to the soup and stir to combine.
Yield: 6 servings

Baked Beans

    2 pounds dried Jacob's cattle beans, navy or pea beans, soaked
    2 cups cold water
    ½ cup molasses
    1 tablespoon dry mustard
    1 large onion, chopped

salt and pepper to taste

In a 6-quart pot or Dutch oven, precook the soaked beans, then drain them well. In a small saucepan, bring the water, salt and pepper, molasses, and dry mustard to a boil, then pour the mixture over the beans. Stir in the onion. Cover and bake the beans for an hour or until tender. Add water if needed to keep the beans moist.

Yield: 8 servings

Bean-and-Vegetable Soup

    1 tablespoon olive oil
    1 medium onion, chopped
    8 to 10 cups of water
    ½ cup uncooked Vermont cranberry beans or navy beans, soaked and then cooked
    2 potatoes, diced
    1 stalk celery, chopped
    ½ pound green beans, cut into pieces
    2 tomatoes, peeled and chopped
    1 leek, green part only, thinly sliced
    salt and pepper to taste

Heat the oil in a large saucepan, add the onion and cook until soft. Add water, then beans, potatoes, celery, and the salt and pepper. Simmer, covered, for 10 to 15 minutes. Add the green beans, the leek, and tomatoes and cook for another 10 minutes.

Yield: 6 servings

Cannellini Bean Purée

    ¼ cup vegetable oil
    1 medium onion, chopped
    2 cloves garlic, minced
    3 cups uncooked cannellini beans, soaked and cooked
    ¼ cup chicken stock
    ¼ cup dry mustard
    4 tablespoons parsley, minced
    salt and pepper to taste

Heat the oil in the skillet, add the onion and garlic and cook until soft. Stir in the mustard. In a food processor, purée the beans with the chicken stock. Add the onion mixture and the parsley. Add salt and

pepper to taste. Pulse until all the ingredients are blended. Heat the purée in a saucepan.
Yield: 6 servings

Refried Beans

    4 tablespoons vegetable oil
    2 cups cooked pinto beans
    3 tablespoons vegetable stock

Heat the oil in a heavy skillet and add the beans. When beans have softened, flatten them with the back of a wooden spoon into a cake. Turn like a pancake and cook through. Top with grated cheddar cheese.
Yield: 4 servings

Split-Pea Soup

    6 cups cold water
    1 medium onion, chopped
    4 large carrots, peeled and chopped
    1 pound smoked ham hock (optional)
    2 cups dried green split peas, rinsed and sorted
    3 cloves garlic, minced
    salt and pepper to taste

In a large saucepan, combine the water and onion, carrots, garlic, and ham hock and bring to a boil. Lower the heat, cover, and simmer for about 1 ½ hours or until the split peas are tender. Remove the ham hock with a slotted spoon. Cut the meat into small pieces and discard the bone. Add the meat to the soup. Add salt and pepper to taste.
Yield: 8 servings.

Black-eyed Peas and Rice

    5 cups cold water
    1 cup black-eyed peas
    1 tablespoon olive oil
    1 medium onion, chopped fine
    1 cup unconverted long-grain rice
    1 garlic clove, minced
    ½ teaspoon red-pepper flakes
    1 small red pepper, chopped

½ teaspoon thyme
1 bay leaf
salt and pepper to taste

In a large saucepan, boil the water, add the peas, and simmer, covered, for about 45 minutes or until beans are tender. In a skillet, heat the oil and sauté the onion and garlic. Add more liquid to the saucepan if necessary. Add the rice, the red-pepper flakes, red pepper, thyme, bay leaf, and salt and pepper. Cook uncovered for 20 minutes or until rice is tender. Turn off heat and let sit for 15 minutes. Remove the bay leaf before serving.

Yield: 4 servings

Herbs & Edible Flowers

105

The Kitchen Gardener's Cookbook

Herbs & Edible Flowers

Peppery smell of nasturtiums. Starched cotton smell of sage. Mint cool as water. Lemon balm. When I weed the herb garden, the scents rise to my nostrils each time my hands touch leaves and stems and fill my head with memories.

I am seven years old and in bed with the mumps, quarantined in my room with only my mother and the doctor as occasional visitors. My oldest sister peeks her head past the door frame once a day and waves hello. When I am a little better, the shades are lifted and sunlight washes the bed where I'm propped up against pillows reading *Mary Poppins*. My mother comes to tidy the room—she rubs the yellow dust cloth over the bookshelves and dresser top and pushes the dust mop over the floor, jabbing at corners and under the bed to rouse the dust. Before she leaves she sprinkles lavender water around the room. A few splashes fall on the open book where Mary Poppins, wind-borne, conveyed by her umbrella, flies over the roof tops.

When I opened the book years later to read it to my daughters, the smell of lavender wafted from the pages as strong as the day my mother sprinkled it over the bed clothes. Suddenly my daughters' and my childhood mingle, our memories of a book and its domestic heroine forever associated with the smell of lavender. I also associate lavender with car and train, boat and airplane trips. My mother always carried smelling salts in her purse—a round bottle of amber-colored granules soaked in golden liquid. One whiff and the car sick, the headachy, the dizzy were restored to health, the undiluted smell of lavender biting into breath, medicinal and strong, the olfactory equivalent of holding a sen-sen on your tongue.

As a tribute to childhood, my mother, and Mary Poppins, I always grow lavender in my herb garden. The silver plants border the bricks that lead to the beds. While the lavender plants remain singular and independent, the mint and lemon balm insist on taking over, and I must pull up whole plants to prevent them from choking less prolific neighbors. I save the leaves to dry and instruct my hands to resist uprooting the plants that grow in thick clusters by the ramblers winding up the shingles by the door. Roses and mint belong together in my mind. Both are so reliable, so necessary to summer. "Go pick some mint," I'd instruct one of my children, and she would go out with a basket, confident of bringing back the right leaves to float in sun tea or lemonade or to garnish bowls of strawberries. Mint, parsley, and chives were the few herbs my family could identify with certainty.

The Kitchen Gardener's Cookbook

My husband never approved of my decision to plant thyme and mint between the terrace bricks so we could smell it when we walked out. He claimed the roots would push the stones apart. But the stones that allowed the thyme and mint to root already had vacancies available. When we moved to the country, I had been surprised by the swatches of purple thyme in the fields. Here was the memory of Thanksgiving and Christmas dinners, vegetable soups simmering on the stove. The first years we lived in our house, I dried the tiny leaves on old window screens and stored them in plastic bags. Gradually, I hammered more nails in the rafters of the garage so I could dry more of the herb garden's yield. Bunches of chive flowers and Egyptian onions dangle from hooks in the kitchen until they fade and gather dust. Southernwood dries in a basket under the kitchen bench so I can stuff it into little muslin bags to hang in closets and place in sweater chests to keep moths away.

My family expresses horror at the manifold uses I find for dried herbs. I use them to repel moths, to chase dog smells from couches and mildew from corners and closets. "What's this?" one will accuse. Extracting a muslin bag of dried leaves from behind a cushion, she'll dangle it by its string as if holding a dead mouse by the tail. I breathe deeply to ascertain the smell. If it's lavender, I am reading *Mary Poppins* or my mother is unscrewing the turquoise cap from the amber bottle and dabbing some of the contents on her handkerchief. If it's mint, the girls are stretched out on chaises, drinking sun-tea, oiling themselves into slickness, oblivious to my warnings about exposure to ultraviolet rays. If it's Southernwood's clean lemon smell, I'm opening the door and walking into the kitchen, calling out, "I'm home!" to the listening house. It's a small container of memories.

Herbs & Edible Flowers

Herbs

Chervil
Growing Tip: Chervil is a good companion to radishes. It increases the radishes' hot flavor.

Cooking Tip: Chervil has a delicate flavor and is good with chicken and fish and egg dishes.

Chives
Growing Tip: Chives are a good companion plant for apple trees because they prevent apple scab.

Cooking Tip: Chives lose their flavor when cooked; use fresh or as garnish. Chives do not dry well but can be freeze-dried. Cut chive stems and place in plastic bags in freezer.

Parsley
Growing Tip: Parsley's flower heads attract beneficial insects. Grow parsley near tomatoes and asparagus. It's also a good companion for roses.

Cooking Tip: Grow several kinds of parsley for different cooking and garnish uses.

Tarragon
Growing Tip: One or two plants are plenty since tarragon spreads.

Cooking Tip: Tarragon can be hung in bunches and air-dried.
For tarragon vinegar, place leafy stalks of tarragon in a glass jar and fill it with white or cider vinegar. Add a few peppercorns and a peeled garlic clove (optional). Screw on lid and put in a sunny place for two weeks. Strain the vinegar into a bottle and throw away the tarragon (optional).

Fines Herbes:
Finely chop equal amounts of chervil, chives, parsley, and tarragon leaves. Mix together and store in air-tight containers.

Mint

Growing Tip: There are many varieties of mint. Spearmint is the most common. Mint flavor is stronger if it is grown in full sun.

Cooking Tip: Cut and hang mint in bunches to dry. Strip leaves from stalks and store them in air-tight containers or plastic bags.

Mint Tea:

2 teaspoons black tea
¼ cup chopped mint
3 ¾ cups boiling water
sugar to taste

Warm a teapot and put in the tea and chopped mint. Pour in the boiling water and leave for five minutes. Pour through a strainer into cups or glasses. Add sugar to taste.
Yield: 4 cups of tea

Mint Sauce:

¼ cup mint, chopped fine
1 teaspoon sugar
2 tablespoons lemon juice
1 tablespoon white-wine vinegar
¼ cup boiling water

Put the chopped mint in a bowl or mortar and mash or pound with sugar until well mixed. Stir in the lemon juice and vinegar, then add the boiling water. Mix well and cool.
Yield: ⅓ cup

Mint Jelly:

2 pounds Granny Smith apples
1 bunch mint
3 ¾ cups water
2 cups sugar
2 tablespoons lemon juice
2 tablespoons white-wine vinegar
¼ cup chopped mint

Wash and chop the apples. Put the apples in a pan with the bunch

Herbs & Edible Flowers

of mint and cold water. Bring to a boil and simmer for about 30 minutes until the apples are soft. Pour into a jelly bag and let drain overnight. Measure the juice and add 2 cups of sugar for every 2 ½ cups of liquid. Bring to a boil in a heavy pan and boil for 20 to 30 minutes until the setting point is reached. Stir in the lemon juice and the vinegar; add the chopped mint. Pour into jars and seal when cool.
Yield: 2 12-ounce jars

Basil

Growing Tip: Don't plant basil near rue. The common basils are purple and green. Like mint, basil is available in flavored varieties such as cinnamon basil and anise basil.

Cooking Tip: Basil is commonly used in tomato and pasta dishes. Pick a bunch and keep it in a jar or pitcher of water to use to flavor casseroles and zucchini dishes.

Pesto:

  2 to 3 cloves garlic
  ½ cup basil leaves
  3 to 4 tablespoons olive oil
  grated Parmesan or Gruyere cheese

In a food processor, finely chop the basil, garlic, olive oil and cheese. If you are using the pesto as a garnish for soup, add a tablespoon of the soup to the pesto as you process it.

Marjoram

Growing Tip: Marjoram is an annual. Bring plants indoors for winter.

Cooking Tip: Sweet or knotted marjoram has the best flavor for cooking. Marjoram is an excellent herb for meat and for zucchini and potato dishes. It is delicious added to the rice in stuffed green peppers.

Oregano

Growing Tip: A close relative of marjoram, their flowers are identical, but oregano's leaves are greener and stronger smelling, and the plant itself is more sprawling.

Cooking Tip: Oregano has a strong flavor. It should be used in hearty dishes. It is excellent for Italian dishes, tomato dishes, and meat loaf.

Rosemary

Growing Tip: Rosemary loves full sun. It needs protection in the winter. Ideally, rosemary plants can be dug up and brought indoors during the cold seasons.

Cooking Tip: Rosemary is delicious with lamb.

Sage

Growing Tip: Rosemary and sage are good plant companions.

Cooking Tip: Sage is a great addition to pâtés, pork dishes, onion dishes, and stuffing.

Sage Stuffing:
- 1 cup dried bread crumbs
- 2 tablespoons chopped onion
- 1 teaspoon dried sage
- ½ teaspoon dried marjoram
- ½ teaspoon dried thyme
- 1 ounce butter melted
- salt and pepper to taste

Mix the ingredients well. If the mixture needs binding, add an egg. For a lighter stuffing, add a little water or milk.

Savory

Growing Tip: Savory grows well with green beans and onions.

Cooking Tip: Savory has a peppery taste and can be substituted for pepper. It is a delicious addition to seafood and to bean dishes.

Thyme

Growing Tip: Garden thyme is the best known of the several varieties of thyme. Try growing thyme in a rock garden.

Cooking Tip: Lemon thyme has a more delicate flavor. Use it in fish dishes or omelets. Use garden thyme in tomato sauce and in meat dishes. Thyme is essential in making a bouquet garni, a seasoning posy.

Herbs & Edible Flowers

Bouquet Garni:
Tie together stems of parsley, thyme, and a bay leaf. Be sure to include more parsley as thyme and bay have strong flavors. Other herbs can be added to the bouquet depending on the dish. Try growing the bouquet herbs together in a container.

Bay
Growing Tip: Bring bay trees indoors during the winter in colder climates.

Cooking Tip: Sweet bay is the only bay that is used in cooking. Use a bay leaf in liquid for poaching fish. Try storing a bay leaf in a jar of rice to give it extra flavor when cooked.

Dill
Growing Tip: Dill seeds are ripe when the plant's flower heads turn brown. Cut plant and continue drying seed indoors.

Cooking Tip: Dill is delicious with fish and with vegetable salads, especially cucumber. Mix dill with cream cheese or butter for a sandwich spread. Use dill in lamb stew and for pickling cucumbers, in vinegars and omelets.

Fennel
Growing Tip: Fennel is a perennial that can grow to be 5 feet tall. It can be grown from seed but requires a long growing season. Finocchio is a variety of fennel with an edible swollen leaf base.

Cooking Tip: Fennel is the "fish herb." Add it to the water for poached or boiled fish. Add chopped fennel leaves to salads and cooked vegetables.

Fennel Salad:
1 large fennel bulb
2 tablespoons olive oil
1 tablespoon white wine vinegar
salt and pepper to taste

Trim the stalks from the fennel bulb and wash the bulb under running water. Slice the bulb across in thin circles, separating them like onion rings. Dry and place in salad bowl. Add the olive oil, vinegar, and salt and pepper to taste.
Yield: 2 servings

Cilantro / Coriander

Growing Tip: The early leaves are cilantro; the later seeds are coriander. Cilantro/coriander likes full sun. It needs a long growing season. For cilantro, pick the leaves as soon as they are fully developed. For coriander, leave the flower heads to go to seed. Cut down the plants in late summer when the seeds have turned light brown. Leave them in a dry place for two to three days. When completely dry, shake out the seeds and store in jars.

Cooking Tip: Ground coriander can be used in cakes and cookies. It is delicious in chutneys. It is important in various spice mixtures like curry. Use coriander seed when making pickles. Use cilantro in salsas and dips.

Cilantro Salsa:

> 4 garlic cloves, minced
> 2 jalapeño chilis, roasted, peeled, seeds removed, and minced
> ½ red pepper, chopped
> 1 cup cilantro leaves
> 1 tablespoon lemon or lime juice
> 1 teaspoon sugar
> ½ teaspoon dried mustard
> 2 tablespoons red-wine vinegar
> 3 tomatoes, quartered, seeded, and drained
> salt and pepper to taste

In a food processor, combine all the ingredients except the tomatoes until coarsely chopped. Add the tomatoes and pulse just enough to chop the tomatoes. Add salt and pepper to taste. Let stand for an hour before draining off excess liquid. Chill before serving.
Yield: 2 ½ cups

Caraway

Growing Tip: Caraway is grown for its seeds and roots only. After the plants flower and before the seed heads burst, cut off the heads and dry. Shake out the seed when completely dry and store in jars. Dig up the roots after the seed heads have been cut.

Cooking Tip: Caraway roots can be boiled and eaten like carrots. Use the seeds in cakes and biscuits.

🌿 Herbs & Edible Flowers

Salad Burnet

Growing Tip: Salad burnet is grown by seed and is self-sowing. This is a good container plant.

Cooking Tip: Salad burnet is used mostly for salads. Use the leaves when they are fresh. Burnet adds a delicious flavor to French dressing. It can be used as a garnish in place of parsley.

Comfrey

Growing Tip: This perennial gets big and is best used as a background plant. It is self-sowing and spreads quickly.

Cooking Tip: Comfrey leaves can be cooked like spinach. Chop the leaves to use in salads. Use only young leaves in cooking.

Cress

Growing Tip: Watercress needs moving water to grow. Land cresses have small leaves and resemble watercress in taste.

Cooking Tip: Use cress fresh in sandwiches and salads or as garnish.

Watercress Soup:
    1 onion, chopped
    4 ounces cress leaves, chopped
    1 pint milk
    salt and pepper to taste
Purée in a food processor. Serve chilled.
Yield: 2 servings

Sorrel

Growing Tip: Sorrel grows in clumps and gets tall. It should be grown as a backdrop planting. Sorrel does not do well in harsh winters.

Cooking Tip: Sorrel is similar to spinach but more acid and sour to taste.

Sorrel Soup:
    ¼ pound sorrel leaves
    ¼ pound lettuce
    2 ½ cups chicken or vegetable stock

The Kitchen Gardener's Cookbook

 1 ½ cups parsley
 ¼ cup butter
 ¼ pound potato
 ¼ cup light cream
 1 teaspoon lemon juice
 salt and pepper to taste

Wash and shred the sorrel and lettuce leaves. Wash and chop the parsley. Heat the butter in a heavy saucepan and add the lettuce, sorrel, and parsley. Cook for 6 minutes then add the peeled and sliced potato. Stir until well mixed, then pour in the stock. Add salt and pepper to taste. Simmer for 25 minutes, then place in food processor and mix until smooth. Add lemon juice and cream and serve.

Yield: 4 servings

Edible Flowers

Edible flowers can be used as effective decoration, as flavoring, and as garnish for certain dishes. They can be grown along the borders of kitchen gardens. Tall flowers can provide a backdrop, or flowers can be sown in their own beds.

Bergamot or **bee balm** has red flowers that add flavor and color to green salads, fruit cups, and fresh fruit salads.

Borage flowers taste like cucumber. Add the leaves and flowers to green salads. Add the flowers to wine.

Borage Tea:

Pour boiling water into a teapot to heat the pot, then pour out the water. Add ½ cup borage leaves and flowers, chopped, to the tea pot and cover with two cups boiling water. Let steep, then strain and serve.

Calendulas' bright yellow petals can be mixed in with scrambled eggs, mixed with rice, or sprinkled on soups.

Herbs & Edible Flowers

Chive blossoms should be cut off to keep the leaves flavorful. Use the flowers in vinegars or as a garnish for vegetable dishes and green salads.

Chive-blossom Vinegar:
Fill a glass jar half full of chive blossoms. Fill with white-wine vinegar. Use a nonmetal cap and put the glass jar in a sunny window. In a week, strain through cheesecloth and dilute with more vinegar.

Daylilies' crunchy, cool-tasting flowers can be dipped in a batter of flour and egg and fried in vegetable oil in a skillet. They can also be added to soups.

Geraniums' delicate flavor refreshes jellies and drinks. Scented geranium leaves can also sweeten jellies and sorbets.

Geranium-leaf Sorbet:
- 12 scented geranium leaves (rose or lemon are good)
- 6 tablespoons sugar
- 1 ¼ cups water
- juice of one lemon
- 1 egg white

Wash the geranium leaves and pat dry. Put the sugar and water in a pan and boil until the sugar has dissolved. Put the leaves in the pan, cover, and turn off the heat. Leave for twenty minutes, strain off the syrup into a container, add the lemon juice, cool, and then freeze until semi-frozen, about 45 minutes to an hour. Fold in stiffly beaten egg white. Freeze for about an hour. Serve in glasses and decorate each glass with a geranium leaf and blossom.

Marigold blossoms should be used when they are fully open. Fresh or dried marigold petals add flavor to rice, cheese, and egg dishes. They also add color to a green salad.

Nasturtiums' bright trumpet-shaped flowers should be eaten young. They are an attractive garnish for green salads. They can be mixed with cream cheese for a dip that must be prepared right before serving.

Sunflower buds can be steamed or boiled to reduce their bitter flavor. They can be added to salads and tossed with vinaigrette.

Violas or **Johnny-jump-ups** are slightly sweet-tasting and are pretty as a decoration for cakes and fruit drinks.

Zucchini blossoms can be stuffed with ricotta or cottage cheese, mixed with chopped onion, chopped parsley, salt and pepper to taste, and baked for 15 minutes.

Index

A
Aioli Sauce, 19
Arugula and Basil Salad, 48
Asparagus, 19-22
Asparagus Bundles, 20

B
Baba Ghanouj, 43
Baked Beans, 99-100
Baked Yellow Peppers
   and Tomatoes, 76
Basil, 111
Bay, 113
Bean-and-Vegetable Soup, 100
Beans. See Dried Beans and
   Shelling Beans; Green Beans
Bee Balm, 116
Beet Horseradish, 24-25
Beets, 23-25
Beets with Onions, 23-24
Beets with Orange and Ginger, 24
Bergamot, 116
Biscuit Pie Crust, 67
Black-Bean Turkey Soup, 99
Black-eyed Peas and Rice, 101-102
Blanching, 3
Borage, 116
Borage Tea, 116
Borscht, 23
Bouquet Garni, 113
Braised Brussels Sprouts, 98
Braised Parsnips, 22-23
Braised Red Cabbage, 85
Broccoli, 36-39
Broccoli Lemon Risotto, 38-39
Broccoli Salad, 37-38
Broccoli Soup, 38
Broccoli Stir-fry, 37
Brussels Sprouts, 97-99
Brussels Sprouts and
   Spinach Salad, 98
Brussels Sprouts with Bacon,
   Onion, and Carrots, 98

Bubble and Squeak, 86
Butternut Bisque, 95
Butternut Squash and
   Cheese Purée, 94-95

C
Cabbage, 84-86
Cabbage Salad, 85
Caesar Salad, 49-50
Calendula, 117
Cannellini Bean Purée, 100-101
Caponata, 45
Caraway, 114
Carrot Cake, 41
Carrots, 39-42
Carrot Salad, 40
Carrot Soup, 41-42
Carrots with Brown Sugar, 40
Cauliflower, 45-47
Cauliflower and Cheese, 47
Cauliflower in Bread Crumbs, 45-46
Cauliflower Salad, 46
Cauliflower Soup, 46
Chaiwalla's Famous Tomato Pie, 67
Chard, 25-26
Chard Soup, 26
Chervil, 109
Chive Blossoms, 117
Chive-blossom Vinegar, 117
Chives, 109
Cilantro, 114
Cilantro Salsa, 114
Coleslaw, 84
Comfrey, 115
Coriander, 114
Corn, 70-74
Corn Bread, 73
Corn Chowder, 73-74
Corn Fritters, 72
Corn-on-the-Cob, 71
Corn Pudding, 72-73
Corn Relish, 74

The Kitchen Gardener's Cookbook

Corn Salad, 72
Cream-Cheese Frosting, 41
Creamed Corn, 71
Creamed Spinach, 79
Cream of Spinach Soup, 80
Cress, 115
Cucumbers, 58-60
Cucumber Salad, 60
Cucumber Soup, 59

D
Daylilies, 117
Dill, 113
Dilled Cucumbers, 61
Dilled Potatoes, 81
Dried Beans and Shelling Beans, 99-102

E
Early Summer, 27-52
Edible Flowers.
 See Herbs & Edible Flowers
Eggplant, 42-45
Eggplant Parmesan, 44
Eggplant Salad, 42
Endive Salad, 48-49

F
Fall, 87-102
Fennel, 113
Fennel Salad, 113
Fines Herbes, 109
Fried Green Tomatoes, 63

G
Garden Salad, 49
Garlic. See Spring Onions and Garlic
Garlic Dressing, 46
Garlic Soup, 18
Gazpacho, 63
Geranium-Leaf Sorbet, 117
Geraniums, 117
German Potato Salad, 81
Ginger Carrots, 40-41
Gratin of Winter Root Vegetables, 93

Green-Bean, Yellow-Pepper,
 and Bacon Salad, 36
Green-Bean and Fingerling-Potato
 Salad, 36
Green-Bean and Radish Salad, 34
Green-Bean Pâté, 33-34
Green Beans, 32-36
Green Beans, Garlic, and Almonds, 33
Green Beans with Ginger, 33
Green-Bean Vinaigrette with
 Red Onion and Dill, 35
Greens, 47-52
Green Salad and
 Goat-Cheese Toasts, 50
Grilled Corn, 70-71
Grilled Eggplant, 42-43
Grilling, 3

H
Herb Dressing, 50
Herbs & Edible Flowers, 103-118

I
Indian Cucumber Salad. *See* Raita

J
Johnny-jump-ups, 117

L
Leek Soup, 17-18
Lemon Carrots with Dill, 40
Lemon Dressing, 79
Lemon and Oregano Dressing, 48
Lettuce Salad with
 Raspberry Dressing, 47-48

M
Marigold Blossoms, 116
Marinated Baby Squash, 69-70
Marinated String Beans, 34
Marjoram, 111
Mesclun Salad, 48
Methods for
 Cooking Vegetables, 3

120

Index

Microwaving, 3
Mint, 110
Mint Jelly, 110-11
Mint Sauce, 110
Mint Tea, 110
Mixed Greens with
   Poppy-Seed Dressing, 51

N
Nasturtiums, 116
New Potatoes and Mint, 83
New Potatoes in Chive Butter, 83

O
Onions. See Spring Onions and Garlic
Onion Tart, 16-17
Orange-Butternut Squash Purée, 95
Orange-Pumpkin Bread, 96
Oregano, 111-112
Oregano Dressing, 48-49

P
Parmesan Asparagus, 19
Parsley, 109
Parsley and Chive Dressing, 49
Parsley and Red-Pepper Dressing, 37-38
Parslied New Potatoes, 80
Parsnip, Garlic, and Potato Purée, 22
Parsnip, Potato, and Garlic Purée, 93-94
Parsnip and Carrot Purée, 23
Parsnips, 22-23
Pasta with Beets, 25
Pasta with Fried Green Tomatoes
   and Chèvre, 64
Pastry Shell, 16, 17
Peas, 11-13
Pea Salad, 12
Peas and Carrots with Pasta, 12-13
Pea Soup, 11
Peas with Bibb Lettuce, 12
Penne with Asparagus
   and Lemon, 21-22
Peppers, 74-77
Peppers and Basil, 77
Pesto, 111

Pickled Cucumbers, 59-60
Picnic Potato Salad, 82
Poppy-Seed Dressing, 51
Potato and Sugar-Snap Peas, 82-83
Potatoes, 80-84
Potato Salad with Arugula, 83-84
Pumpkin au Gratin, 97
Pumpkin Pie, 96
Pumpkins. See Winter Squash and Pumpkins

R
Radish and Cucumber Salad
   with Yogurt, 14-15
Radishes, 14-15
Raita, 59
Raspberry Dressing, 47-48
Ratatouille, 44
Red and Green Salad, 50-51
Red Pepper and Eggplant Dip, 77
Red Pepper Soubise, 75
Refried Beans, 101
Risotto Primavera, 21
Roasted Garlic, 18-19
Roasted Peppers, 76
Roasted Potatoes, 82
Roasted Pumpkin Seeds, 97
Roasted Root Vegetables, 92-93
Romaine and Chicory Salad, 51
Root Vegetables, 92-94
Rosemary, 112

S
Sage, 112
Sage Stuffing, 112
Salad Burnet, 115
Salsa, 65
Sautéed Leeks, 18
Sautéed Peppers, 75
Sautéed Swiss Chard, 25-26
Sautéed Zucchini, 69
Savory, 112
Sesame Zucchini, 70
*Shelling Beans. See Dried Beans
   and Shelling Beans*
Snow Peas and Onion, 13

121

The Kitchen Gardener's Cookbook

Sorrel, 115-116
Sorrel Soup, 115-116
Spiced Broccoli, 37
Spinach, 78-80
Spinach and Bacon Salad, 79
Spinach and Garlic Salad, 78
Split-Pea Soup, 101
Spring, 5-26
Spring Onions and Garlic, 15-19
Spring Onions with Risotto, 16
Steamed Brussels Sprouts with Apples, 99
Steamed Green Beans, 33
Steamed Zucchini, 68
Steaming, 3
Stir-frying, 3
Stuffed Peppers, 75
Stuffed Zucchini, 68
Sugar-Snap Peas, Potatoes, and Chives, 13
Summer, 53-86
Sun-dried Tomatoes, 65
Sunflowers, 117
Sweet and Sour Radishes, 14
Swiss Chard. See Chard
Swiss Chard and Garlic and Penne, 26

T
Tabbouleh, 64-65
Tarragon, 109

Thyme, 112
Tomato, Parsley, and Red-Onion Salad, 62
Tomato Coulis, 62
Tomatoes, 61-67
Tomato Ketchup, 66
Tomato Sauce, 63
Tomato Soup with Tarragon, 66

U
Uncooked Tomato Sauce, 67

V
Vegetable Broth, 94
Violas, 117

W
Warm Cherry-Tomato Salad, 62
Warm Spinach Salad with Arugula, 78
Watercress. See Cress
Watercress and Scallion Salad, 52
Watercress Soup, 115
White-wine Dressing, 60
Winter Squash and Pumpkins, 94-97
Winter-Vegetable Purée, 93

Z
Zucchini, 68-70
Zucchini Blossoms, 117
Zucchini Bread, 69